AMERICAN MARKETING ASSOCIATION

MANAGING
THE
BIG SALE

A Relational Approach to Marketing Strategies, Tactics, and Selling

John V. Crosby

Printed on recyclable paper

NTC Business Books
a division of NTC *Publishing Group* • Lincolnwood, Illinois USA

Library of Congress Cataloging-in-Publication Data
Crosby, John V.
    Managing the big sale: a relational approach to marketing strategies, marketing tac-
tics, and selling/John V. Crosby.
    p.   cm.
    Includes index.
    ISBN 0-8442-3427-3 (alk. paper)
    1. Selling—Key accounts—Management. 2. Sales management.
3. Marketing—Management. I. Title.
HF5438.8.K48C76   1996
658.85—dc20   95-52243
                                                                        CIP

Published by NTC Business Books, a division of NTC Publishing Group
4255 West Touhy Avenue
Lincolnwood (Chicago), Illinois 60646-1975, U.S.A.
©1996 by NTC Publishing Group. All rights reserved.
6 7 8 9 0 BC 0 9 8 7 6 5 4 3 2 1

Contents

Introduction

This is a book about the relational nature of marketing and sales within the broader context of business development. The contents are directly applicable to companies that market and sell products or services to other companies using a well-defined, although complex, sales process. Complex sales differ from the majority of retail or direct consumer sales. In retail or consumer sales, generally only a single customer is involved in the purchase decision and, as such, the sales process is less complex. In the complex sale, several different customers are involved in the decision-making process, and the sale usually cannot be closed without agreement of all of the participants. This complexity, plus the increased length of the selling cycle in a business-to-business environment, requires a well-coordinated approach to planning, market definition, product development, and sales for the process to be most effective.

When the functions of marketing and sales are viewed as relational and interdependent functions rather than separate and often competing entities, the winners will always be the customers! Although often used interchangeably, marketing and sales are very different functions. In the relational model, marketing consists of strategic and tactical elements, and sales largely involves the selling process. The key to effective functioning is in the successful integration of the three components.

In larger companies or companies marketing and selling a large number of product lines, the three functions are generally staffed with several people, each having responsibility for either strategic marketing, tactical marketing, or sales. In smaller organizations or companies with fewer product lines, a single person may satisfy more than one function. Whether your company includes a large, well-differentiated marketing and sales organization or consists of a small staff with each individual wearing many hats, the concepts presented here still apply.

Although the relational model is presented in much detail and is well punctuated with abundant examples and illustrations, this is a conceptual model and should not be applied in a literal cookbook fashion. Throughout the book, examples drawn from companies in the high-tech manufacturing sector are used to illustrate the concepts. Examples drawn from other types of companies would be equally relevant. In the appendix, the basic concepts of the relational model are applied to three radically different types of firms. The model is most appropriate when used as a guide by companies interested in increasing market share, bringing new products to market faster, improving customer satisfaction, developing timely and cost effective technologies, increasing factory utilization, and reducing forecast error.

How to Use This Book

The book is divided into six major parts including the appendix. Part I, "Overview," consists of only one chapter, "The Account Development Cycle and the Complex or 'Big' Sale." This chapter seeks to present the relational nature of strategic marketing, tactical marketing, and sales within the context of business development in general and within the context of the account development cycle in particular. The account development cycle, with its sole focus being the welfare of the customer, is the glue that binds the three functions together in a relational and recursive business process.

Strategic Marketing

Part II, "Strategic Marketing" expands the strategic marketing specialties in five chapters that span topics ranging from role and responsibilities to developing price and promotion strategies. For example, Chapter 2, "The Role, Responsibilities, and Relationships of Strategic Marketing," covers the scope of the function, planning level and horizon, forecast level and horizon, and how information from strategic marketing impacts the company. Chapter 3, "Strategic Planning," identifies strategic marketing as the catalyst for strategic planning and provides a structure for planning and a series of "what-if" questions that are useful in strategic business planning activities. Chapter 4, "Served Markets," develops the concept of served markets and illustrates how various sources of information can be used by the strategic marketer to define and characterize the marketplace and the customers' major needs and wants. Chapter 5, "The Product Portfolio," illustrates how to define the product portfolio and how to communicate the desired information about the features and benefits of the products. Chapter 6, "Market Segmentation," explores various segmentation criteria, defines TAM, SAM, and SOM, and illustrates how profitability goals can influence distribution decisions and how different modes of distribution can influence profitability.

Tactical Marketing

Following strategic marketing, Part III, "Tactical Marketing," consists of four chapters that discusses the tactical marketing specialties in much greater depth. Chapter 7, "The Role, Responsibilities, and Relationships of Tactical Marketing," discusses basic responsibilities and shows how they differ from strategic marketing. This includes planning level and horizon, forecast level and horizon, and how the information generated by tactical marketing impacts the company. Chapter 8, "Market Development," explores product development through the lens of the application matrix. It addresses how the product is positioned and how that positioning is communicated. Chapter 9, "Target Account Identification," illustrates how tactical marketing can further the efforts of marketing and sales by developing a list of accounts that should be targeted. This chapter includes information on various sources that can be called on to help identify these target accounts, how to profile those accounts, identify and profile competitors, and how to construct the all-important sales kit. Chapter 10, "Engagement Strategy," defines the four major types of accounts and illustrates how to employ the sales kit with the appropriate engagement strategy to initiate the sales process.

Sales

Shifting from marketing to sales, Part IV, "Sales," consists of five chapters that range from role and responsibilities, to account qualification and development, to account service and expansion, to technology confirmation. Chapter 11, "The Role, Responsibilities, and Relationships of Sales," completes the definition of the third major function in the model. This chapter includes a discussion of planning level and horizon, forecast level and horizon, and how information generated by sales impacts the company. Chapter 12, "Target Account Qualification," discusses how to apply the engagement strategy, the need to understand the customer's business, and how to identify the most likely sales opportunities to be developed. Chapter 13, "Target Account Development," explains the value in knowing your audience and the leverage to be gained by building relationships early in the selling cycle. It also demonstrates how to link the most appropriate product lines to the defined sales opportunity and how the defined sales opportunity can be tracked through its respective selling cycle. An interesting characteristic of the relational model is that the salesperson is not asked to forecast unconstrained demand or otherwise generate a sales forecast. The salespeople are only asked to define and track their developing opportunities, the marketing functions do the rest. Chapter 14, "Target Account Service and Expansion," addresses the power of satisfying the many customers within a given target account. This includes illustrating how the salesperson must construct a unique service approach for the multiple customers within the account, not just for the company. Chapter 15, "Technology Confirmation," is the process of affirming or influencing the redirection of the company's technologies of choice. This process begins with salespersons chairing a detailed review (with tactical and strategic marketing) as to the success or failure of the account development process in each of their target accounts. This process becomes invaluable as the three functions of strategic marketing, tactical marketing, and sales work together to affirm, define, or redirect the technology direction of the company.

Staying on Track

Clearly an important element of successful marketing and sales organizations is the ability to stay on track or certainly get back on track, if necessary. Part V, "Staying on Track," illustrates how standard software packages like Microsoft Office or Lotus Notes can facilitate the account review and business won/business lost analyses so vital for continued success. Chapter 16, "Target Account Reviews," presents a structured approach to account reviews and describes several ways of approaching such reviews. Chapter 17, "Business Won/Business Lost Analyses," provides additional structure and discussion of a specific type of business review and how this type of review can be conducted. Chapter 18, "Standard Software Tools," explores in detail how Lotus SmartSuite or NotesSuite can be integrated with the account development cycle and the relational approach to strategic marketing, tactical marketing, and sales to yield a powerful electronic and networked reporting system.

Appendix

Three different cases are presented to illustrate the utility and flexibility of the relational model as it applies to markedly different types of companies. Case 1, "Scorpio Sportswear," is a start-up company offering high-end sportswear to specialty markets in the Southwest. Case 2, "Karatchi and Karatchi Legal Services," conveys how the relational model can apply to a professional law firm. The last case, "McGregor's Specialty Meats," describes how the concepts can be applied to a company in the meat processing business.

Part I

Overview

Chapter 1

The Account Development Cycle and the Complex or "Big" Sale

This book is about the complex or "big" sale. This big sale differs from other kinds of selling in several respects. First, it typically is a business-to-business sale. Second, it usually is "big" in the sense that it involves a big price tag. Third, it usually involves several levels of decision makers and several levels of decision making. Fourth, it often involves technologies or processes that are unfamiliar to the buyer or to the customer, although not necessarily. A complex sale might mean the sale of a computer system to an industrial company, but it also might mean the sale of 100,000 shirts to a major retailer. In either case, the process is complex and the stakes are high. Fifth, a big sale also involves several different presentations before the sale is closed; the process of closing this kind of sale can take months or even years. And, sixth, after-sale service of a big sale usually is much more extensive than for other types of sales. It is, virtually, a process unto itself.

This book is about some of the most frequently heard comments in marketing and sales departments. Namely:

- Why don't the salespeople stay on track? Why do they bother with marginal accounts?
- How are we supposed to put promotion programs and sales kits together with this kind of information? And, why don't the sales-people use these kits?

- How are we supposed to sell this kind of product, at that kind of price, to our kinds of customers?

These and hundreds of questions like them often characterize the working relationship between marketing and sales or, more specifically, among those who develop marketing strategies (marketing), marketing tactics (communications and sales support), and the sales force.

Relationship Marketing, Relationship Selling, and the Account Development Cycle

Lots of books have been written about *relationship marketing* and *relationship selling*. But few of them provide any help for managing the process of the big sale; namely, the development of a marketing strategy that can be translated into marketing tactics that in turn can help identify sales targets and close the sale. The reason is that these books focus on the relationship between the marketer and the customer or the salesperson and the customer. They do not deal with the complex internal relationship between and among all of the internal forces that contribute to making a sale. In other words, they do not view marketing and sales as a business process.

The term *process* has been used several times already. And it will be used quite often throughout this book because the complex or big sale requires a process that integrates and coordinates the efforts of marketing strategists, marketing tacticians, and salespeople. While every marketing and sales situation undoubtedly would benefit from such coordination, the complex sale *demands* it because, by the nature of the sale, the customer demands it. The process for managing the complex sale is the Account Development Cycle, which will be the subject of much of this book. Basically, the Account Development Cycle is the process used to manage marketing strategy and tactics and the sales effort on a relational basis. The focus of this process is the exchange and use of information that enables the company to meet the short-term, mid-term, and long-term needs of its customers.

Marketing and Sales: Some Working Definitions

The terms *marketing* and *sales* are often used interchangeably, but, especially in the context of a complex sale, they are not the same. Marketing involves a long planning horizon and, broadly speaking, is primarily responsible for such functions as: the definition of technologies, identification of products and services, delineation of served markets, product positioning, product pricing, and the definition and achievement of specific revenue and profit goals. Sales, on the other hand, has a much narrower focus and utilizes marketing's plans and analyses to call on identified prospective accounts, build personal relationships with qualified buyers, identify specific opportunities, close sales, and provide ongoing service to each of the many customers within the target accounts. In addition, salespeople provide a valuable view of the current marketplace through their day-to-day interaction with the customer. Clearly, the two functions are different, yet they are interdependent.

To be successful, marketing and sales must function relationally, which means that the roles and responsibilities of each are defined in terms of the other's needs and from the perspective of the customer. For example, because the primary role of sales is to sell products and services at a level of price, quality and performance acceptable to the customer, the sales force can be successful only if the roles and responsibilities of marketing are defined and practiced in a manner complementary to both sales and the customer. By the same token, if marketing's primary role is to deliver profit and market share for the company, then the role of sales must be defined in a manner complementary to both marketing and the customer; in other words, to find and service customers who want the company's products and services. When viewed relationally, the question of what constitutes a satisfied customer or a successful marketing or sales organization shifts away from looking at one or the other function and, instead, focuses on the patterns of interaction that take place between marketing and sales in response to customers' needs. Of course, these "hard-edged" role definitions vary from organization to organization and from industry to industry. This is a dynamic process and, as such, varies with specific needs and demands.

As the level of interaction increases and the relationship between marketing and sales strengthens, the level of complexity increases significantly. While specific time frames and functions vary with the specific industry, the levels of responsibility, detail and different views of the future do not. Sales tends to focus on the immediate or very near term while marketing tends to take the longer view. A good rule of thumb for strategic marketing's planning horizon is 5 to 10 years; for tactical marketing, 1 to 3 years; and for sales, the current fiscal year.

Successful Interdependence

Relationships are the building blocks of success. When strong and effective relationships are in place, ideas and differences of opinion that might be viewed as competitive and divisive are transformed into advantages. Organizations that take the time to create a climate that encourages the building and nurturing of relationships are much more likely to weather adversity and change than those that do not. Successful interdependence occurs when marketing is dependent on sales and the customer; sales is dependent on marketing and the customer; and the customer is dependent on both. Each function acts upon and in turn is acted upon by the others in recursive patterns of interaction.

The Account Development Cycle

The account development cycle (Exhibit 1.1) describes the process of integrating the efforts and information of marketing strategy, market tactics, and sales. It is used to manage marketing and sales within the wider context of business development. As a cyclical and recursive process, it moves from strategic planning to market development to

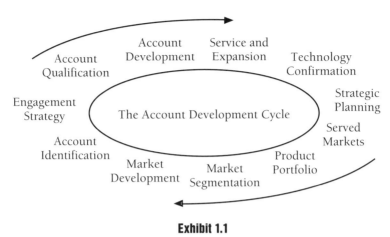

Exhibit 1.1

The Account Development Cycle: An Overview

target account development to target account service and expansion and back to strategic planning. Each of the steps in the cycle has its own patterns of interaction with feedforward and feedback loops that will be explored in subsequent chapters. This approach develops the value and contributions of the specialized disciplines and subdisciplines of marketing and sales, as well as the relationships between them.

Strategic Marketing

The primary responsibilities of strategic marketing include *strategic planning*, definition of *served markets*, creation of the *product portfolio*, and *market segmentation* (Exhibit 1.2). Satisfying these primary areas involves working within a planning horizon of five to ten years and includes defining specific product lines or product groups, conducting market and marketing research, segmentation studies, developing descriptions of likely product applications, conducting major competitive analyses, and generating a broad range of pro forma financials. Implicit in this approach are discussions and decisions about current and projected technologies that will be needed to realize the projected goals and objectives of the business plan.

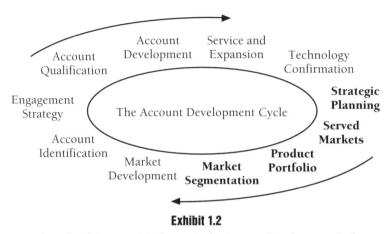

Exhibit 1.2
The Role of Strategic Marketing in the Account Development Cycle

Tactical Marketing

While strategic marketing has primary responsibility for the definition of served markets, tactical marketing has the primary responsibility for *market development* (Exhibit 1.3). Market development typically takes the form of expansion, contraction, or redefinition of one or more of the served market segments. For example, strategic marketing may have originally defined the served market for color laser printers as consisting mainly of networked desktop applications. Tactical marketing, working with sales, may discover new information showing that there are growth and profit opportunities if the served market application is redefined to include the individual home-based professional.

Tactical marketing is also primarily responsible for *account identification* and *engagement strategy*. A broad selection of electronic data sources is available to help identify prospective target accounts. Marketing tacticians screen the "long list" of possible customers to produce a short list of prospective target accounts for sales, saving an incredible amount of time and money.

Once the short list of prospective target accounts has been generated, marketing tacticians prepare detailed target account profiles including the identification of the most likely competitors. These profiles identify each target account in terms of size, product lines,

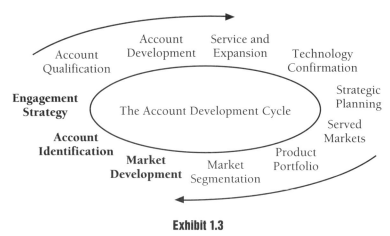

Exhibit 1.3
The Role of Tactical Marketing in the Account Development Cycle

markets served, share-of-market by product line, position in the marketplace, profitability, major customers by product line, major competitors by product line, management structure, key personnel by function, and potential sales opportunities by product line. These profiles are combined with product data sheets, marketing communications, and positioning materials to form the sales kits. The sales kits are used by marketing tacticians to train the salespeople. These materials help the salespeople understand the engagement strategy and how the critical features and benefits of the various products and product lines can help them plan how to engage their respective accounts.

Sales

Sales is responsible for *account qualification, account development, account service and expansion* and *technology confirmation* (Exhibit 1.4). Account qualification defines the process of contacting and meeting with various key people within the target account to understand and quantify their respective needs and wants. The qualification process also determines the importance and urgency of the needs and wants and assesses whether or not the opportunities being discussed have been funded. Once the account is qualified, the process of account development can proceed.

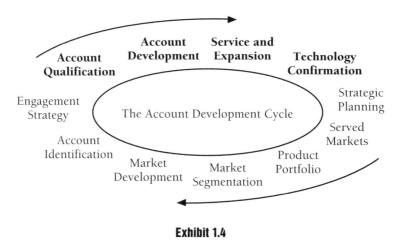

Exhibit 1.4

The Role of Sales in the Account Development Cycle

The early stages of the account development process may take several weeks or several months, depending on the complexity of the products and whether the target account is a new or existing account and whether the products are new or existing. For example, if it is a new account, then the salesperson must build the basic confidence of the decision makers by acquainting them with the company. After building the necessary relationships, the salesperson identifies and quantifies one or more specific sales opportunities, makes the appropriate presentations and tracks each opportunity through its respective selling cycle. Generally, different product lines require somewhat different selling cycles. Knowing where each opportunity is in the selling cycle can be very useful when the salesperson is asked to submit a bookings forecast.

Account service and expansion follow the sale. With complex sales, the key to effective service is to first understand the many different and often competing expectations of the various customers within the account. It is essential to understand what is important to the key people and to structure the service review around those expectations. The concept of service is different for different accounts and might include monthly or quarterly meetings where summary statistics on quality, delivery, price changes, stocking requests, and inventory positions are presented. Wherever possible, the use of graphs is recommended.

Asking salespeople to be responsible for technology confirmation or redirection may seem strange, but this is a neglected area. The salespeople are usually very knowledgeable about how their company's products and services satisfy or do not satisfy the needs and wants of the marketplace. Unfortunately, few companies have an effective means of gathering this valuable information. The account review process can be the vehicle for gathering such information.

Regularly held account reviews include a detailed business won/business lost analysis for each of the sales opportunities identified. Sharing information with sales, tactical marketing, and strategic marketing provides a unique opportunity to discuss what is working well and what requires improvement. This discussion provides the opportunity to reaffirm or redirect the strategies and tactics being used.

Part II

Strategic
Marketing

Chapter 2

The Role, Responsibilities, and Relationships of Strategic Marketing

When viewed as a relational process, the functions of strategic marketing, tactical marketing, and sales all have primary and secondary roles in the business development process. The role and primary responsibilities of strategic marketing and its relationship to tactical marketing and sales are the focus of this chapter.

The Role of Strategic Marketing

The primary role of strategic marketing is to develop the long look ahead and communicate that look to the wider organization and, specifically, to tactical marketing. Together, the two marketing functions continually view both the present and the future. An equally important role of strategic marketing is to learn from the marketplace feedback gained through the organization's business won/business lost analyses and quarterly account reviews. Staying in touch with the marketplace enables marketing strategists to determine the outcome of their plans. In other words, did the critical events occur as planned? Where they close? Where they far different?

Major Responsibilities

Major responsibilities for strategic marketing include identifying the many possible served markets for the company's products and services and discussing the relationship of the markets served currently to those anticipated for the future. It includes defining new products and services for each of the served markets together with the required technologies and product development pathway. Strategic marketing is also responsible for defining the profitability and share-of-market goals for each of the major product lines anticipated. This includes anticipated selling prices and cost targets that must be met at critical milestones if the projected profitability and share-of-market goals are to be realized. Strategic marketing's responsibilities also include defining criteria for the selection of prospective target accounts. This includes profiling the most likely competitors and providing an estimate of their response to the company's planned activities.

Although strategic marketing is almost always viewed from the perspective of positive growth, the perspective of defensiveness is equally important. A key responsibility of strategic marketing's long look ahead is to detect any potential threat to the company's employees, physical facilities, technologies, products, services, and markets and to devise solutions.

Relationship to Tactical Marketing and Sales

Strategic marketing has a direct relationship to tactical marketing and sales and an indirect relationship to customers. For example, its relationship to tactical marketing involves the feedforward of information about the products and services anticipated for each future served market. This includes analysis of the appropriate price and cost points that must be met if the revenue, margin, and share-of-market goals are to be met.

Tactical marketing's relationship to strategic marketing is to provide feedback regarding desirable refinements to existing products and services, customer satisfaction in each of the served markets, actual versus planned market penetration, what the competition is doing, confirmation of projected price and cost trends, and the actual position of each major product line relative to its planned position.

Strategic marketing's major relationship to sales consists mainly of listening and learning about the current marketplace and what is working and not working. Detailed business won/business lost analyses are presented and discussed during regularly held account reviews. These analyses include information about the sales kit, selling cycle, customers needs and wants, served markets, products, applications, pricing, competition, quality, reliability, lead times, and customer service. When effective relationships are in place and representatives of strategic marketing, tactical marketing, and sales are present during the account reviews, an incredible number of issues can be addressed in a remarkably short time period.

Scope

The term *scope* indicates the level of detail involved in strategic marketing's planning efforts. The scope is necessarily restricted and involves the projection of activities some five to ten years into the future. Typically, planning involves the broad definition of technologies needed to manufacture the planned products at the quality and cost levels required by the served markets as well as the definition of new product groups to be designed.

Planning Level and Horizon

In terms of products, the planning level of strategic marketing is restricted to the product group or the product family. Expected quantities and their dollar value are derived from market growth rates and share-of-market assumptions. This takes advantage of the principle of aggregation, using product mix and market research data, and provides ample leeway for tactical marketing planners to expand the planning process as new information becomes available.

An example of product planning would be the definition of a new family of high-speed modems for the rapidly growing telecommunications market. The trend has been toward faster and faster modems, while the price per bit transmitted has dropped precipitously. The volume of the new product family could be estimated from the growth rates of the current modem market plus the rate at which the Internet is growing. Speed, cost per bit transmitted, expected selling price, and desired market share will determine whether existing technology can satisfy customers or whether new technologies will be required.

The planning horizon for strategic marketing is typically five to ten years. This means a minimum of a five-year revenue and profit plan is required for each of the major product families involved. If new technologies are to be developed, the five-year plan must take that into consideration and show the source and application of funds to pay for the new development. Planned cost reductions would also have to occur for the margin goals to be met. The plan would also describe the slope of the cost improvement curve.

Forecast Level and Horizon

Forecasting, at the strategic marketing level, must include knowledge of what's happening in the national economy. The following questions must be considered: How is the economy structured? Which micro-sectors of the economy contain data about our products? What will be the relationship of the projected product groups or product families to the national economy? Will the product family move in a procyclical fashion or will it move in a more contracyclical manner? What will be the impact of any recessionary periods that may occur while we bring the new products to market?

The forecast should be in seasonally adjusted constant dollars to agree with the U.S. Government data and to control for the effects of inflation. Constant dollars can then be converted to current dollars using the Implicit Price Deflator. Two key concepts that are useful in forecasting are the Average Recession Recovery Model and the Average Experience Model.

The Average Recession Recovery Model (ARRM)

The Average Recession Recovery Model (ARRM) is a powerful forecasting tool that can be used to understand how a particular phase of the business cycle is performing versus its average performance over the past fifty years or so. ARRM is ideally suited for the strategic marketer because it provides a pattern of the particular parameter being forecast and provides the greatest amount of information about a particular segment of the economy.

The ARRM usually averages data from the nine prior post–World War II recessions or recoveries. The ARRM shown in Exhibit 2.1 is the Industrial Production Index (IPI). In the graph, the solid line (ARRM9) is the average performance of the IPI across all nine postwar recoveries and indexed to 100 in the second quarter of 1991, the trough of the 1990 to 1991 recession. Against this line, we super-

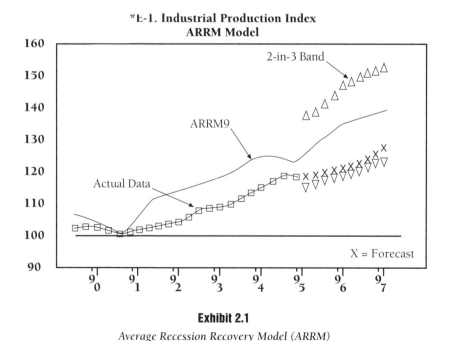

Exhibit 2.1

Average Recession Recovery Model (ARRM)

impose the boxed line of actual data in this tenth business cycle. The closer the two lines are to one another, the more representative the new cycle is to the average of the prior cycles. The two lines of small triangles above and below the solid ARRM9 line describe the plus-and-minus-one standard deviation of the historical data. These two lines can be interpreted as a band within which approximately two out of three of the historical observations fall. The line with the Xs represents the forecast for the current cycle.

ARRMs can also be constructed from data at the level of industry group, product group, product family, or product line. This capability becomes very useful, for example, when the strategic marketer is interested in understanding the relationship of specific product groups to industry averages. Similar concepts can be applied to forecasting sales of new product families using another model called the Average Experience Model.

The Average Experience Model (AEM)

The Average Experience Model (AEM) makes use of concepts similar to those of the ARRM. The key difference here is that knowledge from prior new product introductions are first seasonally adjusted and then indexed to a common introduction point. Usually, a family of curves is generated. At first, the forecast is the average of the prior introductions. As new information becomes available for the current introduction, the forecast is adjusted accordingly.

Impact of Information

Of the three functions, the information generated by strategic marketing has the greatest impact on the future of the organization. This information is used by senior management to drive major expansion or contraction decisions including the opening or closing of factories, strategic partnering, mergers, acquisitions, or divestitures. The weight given to the information generated by strategic marketing is incredible. Basically, top management is betting the organization's future on how accurately their strategic marketing people view the future! The long lead times involved in this type of planning can exacerbate the inherent problems, however, especially if strong and effective relationships are not in place between strategic marketing, tactical marketing, and sales.

Chapter 3

Strategic Planning

Our view of effective business planning includes both the process of planning and the content of planning. The *process* of planning is highly interactive and involves the generation of ideas through rich dialogue prompted by three broad questions: Where are we now? Where would we like to be by when? and How do we get there? The *content* of the plan is created from the planning process dialogue, and planning areas are prioritized according to the operating environment of the business. The planning content may include some or all of the following areas:

- Your company
- Industry information
- Management team
- Total market
- Market segments served
- Marketing
- Products/services
- Sales
- Operations
- Research and development
- Human resources
- Risks and contingencies
- Financials
- Supporting materials

A Catalyst For Planning

When marketing and sales are viewed as a relational process, strategic marketing is the catalyst for business planning because effective business planning is in fact a dynamic narrative about those factors of greatest interest to the organization's members. As a dynamic narrative, the business plan must be, not the sole responsibility of marketing strategists, but the collective responsibility of all participating members of the business. Functioning as a catalyst, however, the marketing strategist can present a number of different scenarios about the future, based on different assumptions. These scenarios can then serve as discussion points around which the planning process can proceed.

Business planning is most effective when viewed as a recursive "what-if" process rather than as a checklist of activities to be completed. Viewed in this way, the planning process serves as the all important crucible for the creation of effective relationships. The plan itself simply consists of the documentation of those agreements, decisions, concerns, and conclusions that have the most relevance for the participants. The plan is a summary statement of the major strategies, tactics, and timelines agreed to during the planning process and documents how the organization collectively envisions the future.

Critical Questions

Following are some of the broad business issues that can be addressed in business planning:

- What are the marketplace and the market segments served by our company?

- How do each of us, and other members of the management team, compare against our competition? What are our key strengths and assets? How can we amplify and capitalize on our strengths and assets? What makes us unique?

- How clear, to us and our customers, are the descriptions of the features and benefits of the products or services we offer?

- What is the size of the total market and each of the market segments served?

- What is the quality of our existing products? What is the product history? What are the trends? Can we deliver the required quality with existing technology, or must we upgrade our technology and improve our business practices to remain competitive?

- What are the current selling prices for our goods and services? Are they holding steady? Going down? Historically, what has been the slope of the selling price curve for those products that account for 80 percent of our revenue? How do our prices relate to those of our competition? How do we know?

- How many competitors do we have? Are they increasing or decreasing? What are their strengths and weaknesses compared to ours? What can we expect them to do in response to our planned activities?

- Should we build another plant or store? If so, where?

- How much can we spend? Will our projected sales growth support a new facility?

- What do we want our roles to be, moving forward? Should we organize functionally or by department? By process technology? By team? By type of customer? Geographically? Centralized or decentralized?

- What gross and net margins can we expect? What margins do we need? How do the two compare?

- What is our revenue per employee? How does this figure compare with our competition's? What is our target? What is their target?

- What product mix should we have? At what volume?

- What are our planning procedures? How do they compare with those of our competition?

- What are the critical risks we face? How can we anticipate them?

This list contains just a few of the many questions a business plan can answer. A great many other questions can also serve as valuable discussion points as the future of the business is constructed through dialogue. Looking at the whole, both the process and the content of business planning provide a tremendous opportunity to share perspectives, organize thoughts, identify and share concerns, and plan for the future. Perhaps most important, the planning process provides an opportunity to develop the all-important relationships that are necessary for success. In the following sections we will look at each of the key elements of business planning in more detail.

Key Elements of the Business Plan

Although the process and content of business planning varies based on the needs and wants of the participants, a few key elements should be discussed in any effective dialogue about the future. This chapter

---

Checklist 1
Key Business Planning Elements

- Statement of your company and what distinguishes it from the other companies in your field
- Information about the industry of which your company is a part
- The management team and the organization structure
- The total market organization and structure
- Market segments served by your company
- Marketing plan
- Products/services provided by your company
- Sales plan
- Operations plan
- Research and development plan
- Human resources plan
- Critical risks and contingencies plan
- Historical and pro forma financials
- Supporting materials

---

will discuss what each of the key elements is intended to address, suggest how the information can be generated, and illustrate how the information can be useful as you seek to chart the future course of your business.

Statement of Your Company

The statement of your company should be a clear, crisp statement that accurately and succinctly describes your company and how it differs from the other companies with whom you compete. The statement should be worded in a way that will help other people understand its message. The following areas should be covered in your company statement:

- A description of the business in which your company is engaged
- The history of your company and of its founders

Checklist 2

Questions for Formulating Your Company Statement

1. What business or businesses are you in?
2. If it is a new venture, what is the motivation for starting the business?
3. If it is an existing business, why was it started? How was it started?
4. What is the early history of the company? Who were the founders and what was their business philosophy?
5. What were the early products and how successful were they?
6. How were those early products or services defined, developed, and sold?
7. Who were the initial customers? Are they still customers? Why? Why not?
8. How are your current products the same or different from earlier products?
9. How do potential customers learn about you and your products?

- The major products or services offered
- Your major customer segments and their related business fields
- A description of how your products or services differ from the competition
- A brief statement of your company's leadership position in the industry
- A statement of the charter or mission of your company

Information about the Industry

The next element of business planning is to develop a historical perspective on your industry. The more people know about the major trends occurring within the industry, the more they are able to contribute their perspectives on the future. For example, what were the early major events that helped shape your industry? Were they serendipitous? What are the major trends that are emerging currently and how do they impact product features? Are cost and price considerations driving product integration? Does your industry lead or lag the general economy? Does your company lead or lag the industry? How do your industry trends relate to national economic trends? The following areas should be explored:

Checklist 3

Questions for Developing the Company's Historical Perspective

1. What trade associations maintain information on the history of the industry?

2. Which major stock brokerage firms have market analysts who follow your industry?

3. Which newspapers and magazines have trend information? For example, special articles could be used to help identify significant events or describe new technologies.

4. How can this information be integrated with the specific company data to help you develop your view of the future?

- A short history of your company's industry and the industries in which it markets its products
- Major events, and their timing, that helped shape your industry
- The major leaders in the industry and the market segments served by your company
- The major trends emerging in the various segments
- The relationship of import and export activities to government regulations
- The opportunities and challenges faced by your company as society becomes more information and services dominated
- The impact of global politics on the success of your company

Management Team and Organization Structure

As the demand for the company's products and services increases, additional employees will be hired. Some of the new employees will assume some of the duties and responsibilities of existing personnel while others will be hired to assume newly created functions. It is often helpful in the enculturation of new employees to describe the management team, team members' backgrounds, and their management philosophy and operating style. It is also helpful to describe the organization's formal structure and explain the reasons for being organized as you are. For example, if your company must compete largely on price, you may be organized functionally as a means of controlling costs. If, on the other hand, time-to-market and market penetration are more important, then perhaps you are organized into strategic business units (SBUs).

The following areas should be included in this element:

- Description of the backgrounds, education and major accomplishments of the key personnel
- Statement of the management team's philosophy and operating style
- Statement and short discussion of the management team's strengths and weaknesses and what makes them unique
- Statement and short discussion of the management team's ethics and general approach to business

---

Checklist 4

Questions for Describing the Management Team and Organization Structure

1. Who are the key players? What are their backgrounds? What are their strengths and assets?

2. How do they compare against your major competitors' management teams?

3. How do the structure and reporting relationships of the management team help the company achieve its goals and objectives?

4. What are the major challenges facing the organization in the next three to six months, six to twelve months, one to three years, and three to five years?

5. How are decisions made?

6. What type of information is used to help manage and grow the business?

7. How are new management people attracted to and brought into the company?

- Statement of how employees are to be compensated, such as stock, profit sharing, straight salary, bonuses, and so on

- Discussion about how employees enter and leave the organization

Market Organization and Structure

As we begin to address market issues, it might be helpful to spend a few minutes and develop a shared vocabulary.

Total Available Market (TAM). The *total available market* describes the broader market which is usually subdivided into many smaller and more specific segments. For example, if your company manufactures and sells notebook computers, the served market might be portable computers, but the TAM would be electronic computers.

The structure and organization of the markets influence how your products and services are marketed and sold. How is the market segmented? What are the major segments? How were they determined? Who are the major competitors by segment? In our example, the TAM for electronic computers might be segmented further into large-scale general-purpose computers, mid-range general-purpose computers, personal computers and workstations, portable computers, and other computers. In this example, the markets are structured around types of computers rather than around types of applications.

Served Available Market (SAM). The *served available market* refers to that portion of the total available market that is defined by the products and services sold by your company. When your company is active in one or more market segments, it is important to look at both TAM and SAM to get a sense of how big a player your company is in the overall scheme of things.

Share-of-Market (SOM). Determining *share-of-market* is always important. A small share of market in a rapidly growing market segment means that you will probably encounter a growing number of competitors. A large share of market in a slower-growing market segment means your company's product lines can grow only as fast as the market segment. To be most accurate, define SOM as a percent of the served available market (SAM) and not as a percentage of the total available market (TAM).

The following areas should be included in your analysis of market organization and structure:
- Define the size and annual growth rates of each of the total markets of interest
- Define the major trends or developments that are occurring in the markets and understand how they could impact your company and the markets it serves
- Understand the major economic factors and how they influence the markets
- Define and understand the cyclical or noncyclical nature of the markets
- Understand how those indicators that lead or lag your company's revenues can be used to give you a competitive advantage
- Understand the growth rates of the markets and how they relate to the desired growth of your company

---

Checklist 5

Questions for Developing the Market Analysis

1. Are the overall markets shrinking or expanding? What are the estimates or forecasts for future growth?

2. What factors seem to be driving the markets?

3. What factors or changes in the market could result in major market shifts? For example, are there factors that could threaten your markets as they are known today? How about factors that might result in explosive growth?

4. What are the national and international trends influencing your markets?

5. What is the lead/lag relationship between the economy and your markets?

6. What major societal trends have the potential of influencing your markets?

7. Which companies dominate the market? What do you know about them, their products, their service, their customers, and their management?

Market Segments Served by Your Company

Markets can be segmented any way you wish. One thing to keep in mind, however, is that how you segment your markets can impact the availability and use of marketing research information. For example, if you segment your markets differently than your competitors do or differently than the industry association to which you belong, then you may not be able to make direct comparisons of the marketing data. Privately funded marketing research information can become very expensive. When in doubt how to segment, it is helpful to review your association's statistics and review how the federal government has segmented your markets.

The following steps should be taken in determining your market segments:

• Identify the major customers served and categorize their applications

---

Checklist 6

Questions for Identifying Market Segments

1. What are the criteria that define your customers? Are these criteria the same for all segments?
2. What factors influence the segments served by your company? Are the segments expanding, shrinking, or staying the same?
3. What do you know about your competitors' products and product lines?
4. What are the major benefits expected by your major customers?
5. What is the relationship between the expected benefits and the product features?
6. What are the opportunities for product integration?
7. What strengths and assets within your company can be used to further differentiate your company from the competition?

- Identify your major competitors and their major products and product lines
- Review the trade press to see what segment names are being used
- Estimate the size and growth rate of each segment
- Define potential share-of-market for each segment served
- Define any seasonal factors, such as holidays, that might dominate the segments
- Project how different segments can be integrated using additional products

Marketing Plan

The marketing plan is your company's road map for the future. It consists of both strategic and tactical elements and serves as the foundation for all subsequent planning activities. The sales plan is generated from the marketing plan. Factories are sized and people are hired based on operations management's interpretation of the marketing plan. New technologies are funded and research projects initiated based on the projected product line performance and cost forecasts contained in the marketing plan. The marketing plan is the pivotal element in the business planning process.

Strategic Marketing The catalyst in the business planning process is strategic marketing. Marketing strategists are expected to take the lead in developing the long look ahead. The more specialized functions of market research, marketing research, and marketing communications are subordinate to the broader functions of strategic and tactical marketing.

The following steps should be taken in preparing your strategic marketing plan:

- Develop a solid data-based approach for your plans and projections
- Place your plans in context by presenting recent history as a bridge to the future
- Illustrate and explain how your marketing plan ties in or does not tie in with the major trends in the market
- Briefly show how the research data were gathered and analyzed
- List your assumptions and describe how specific conclusions were reached

---

Checklist 7

Questions for Preparing the Strategic Marketing Plan

1. Can your assumptions be validated by focus groups conducted by your marketing research people?
2. Of your targeted accounts, which ones are opinion leaders? Are they also early adopters? Are they cooperative?
3. Are systems in place to track the activities of your major competitors?
4. What companies are active in your planned areas? Are they open to partnering, joint ventures, or strategic alliances?
5. What are the required levels of product quality and reliability?

- State the criteria for selecting your key customers and major accounts
- Describe the broad application categories envisioned for each market segment
- Discuss your broad strategy for engaging major types of accounts
- Identify your major competitors by market segment and briefly describe their expected response to your plans
- Define your general pricing and cost strategies
- Describe the size and growth rates for each segment together with your share-of-market assumptions
- Generate a revenue forecast for each segment that supports your previous assumptions
- Build a strong dialogue with tactical marketing throughout the entire process

Tactical Marketing. The focus of tactical marketing is in the present and the near future. As discussed previously, tactical marketing's primary responsibilities are to implement the strategic initiatives, develop the current and next generation products, identify the target accounts, set prices, establish the engagement strategy, develop the sales kit, and train the field sales force. Tactical marketing makes the marketing plan happen.

The tactical marketing plan should include the following areas:

- Understand the product development strategies
- Understand and apply the target account selection criteria
- Validate the product performance profiles
- Develop product features and benefits data sheets
- Establish price and cost objectives for each product
- Develop an operating forecast by product type in units and dollars
- Expand the competitor profiles
- Establish the engagement strategy for each of the prospective target accounts
- Develop the sales kit and define the selling cycle for each product line

---

Checklist 8

Questions for Developing the Tactical Marketing Plan

1. What is the current status of your major competitors?
2. Are your products performing as planned? What secondary development activities can be exploited?
3. Are your product price and cost targets still valid?
4. What is your share of market for each product line? How do they compare with the plan?
5. Are the selling cycles accurate?
6. What is the feedback from the account reviews? Are the engagement strategies working? Are the sales kits working? Are you winning the accounts as planned?
7. What is the price elasticity for each product line?
8. Are the product applications developing as planned?

- Use the sales kit and the selling cycle to explain the engagement strategy and train the sales people

Products/Services Provided by Your Company

Your analysis of the products and services offered by your company should answer the following questions. What are the major product groups or product families manufactured and/or sold by your company? Are the groups defined in such a way that people understand which market segments they serve? How do your product groups relate to those of your competition? If different, how different and why are they different? How are they the same? How do they relate to your industry association groupings?

The following areas should be included in your product/service analysis:

- Description of your company's product/service families or categories
- Discussion of the relatedness of the product families

Checklist 9

Questions for Developing the Product/Services Analysis

1. How were the product groups defined? Were they defined by the industry or were they defined by the customer base?

2. Are the product groups also categorized by application? Are they categorized by major type of customer? How are the products organized? What is the purpose of the organization?

3. How clear are the features and benefits for each of the product groups? Do existing customers recognize similar benefits? How do the product features relate to the benefits?

4. What are your customers' perception of your products' or services' quality and/or reliability? For what reasons do the customers like or dislike your products?

5. Who are your major competitors? What are their strengths and weaknesses? How do their plants or stores operate?

6. How are your products differentiated from those of your competition?

7. Where are each of your major products in the product life cycle? What information is available on customer returns? Warranties? Competitive comparisons? Customer complaints? Failure analysis reports?

- Discussion of the position of your products in the product life cycle
- Discussion of the competitive features of your company's products or services
- Statement and discussion of the quality and reliability of your company's products or services
- Description and discussion of the preferred types of applications for your company's products
- Discussion of critical patents or other legal advantages that might be exploited

Sales Plan

The primary goal of sales is to focus on the development, penetration, and service of each of the prospective target accounts identified by marketing. Sales people should not spend their valuable time prospecting or otherwise trying to identify prospective customers within their territories. Sales people are not equipped for efficient prospecting, marketing people are! Because the marketing people conceive and develop the product, they are best qualified to describe the customer. Because they develop the engagement strategy, they are most qualified to identify the prospective customers. The sales people are to develop relationships with the customers within each of the target accounts, identify the targeted opportunities, and move the customer through the product selling cycle to a mutually successful close.

The following items should be part of the sales plan:

- Size the sales force using the product line mix, revenue, cost and share-of-market goals projected by marketing
- Using the prospective target accounts identified by tactical marketing, develop a revenue plan for each of the major product lines for each of the target accounts

---

Checklist 10

Questions for Developing the Sales Plan

1. How does the selling cycle differ across product lines?
2. Are experts on staff for each of the major product line selling cycles?
3. What is the close ratio for each product line?
4. How much could the selling expenses be reduced if the close ratio were to be reduced, for example, from 1:4 to 1:3?
5. What is the salesperson turnover? What is your competitors' turnover?
6. Do you give your salespeople incentive to generate accurate forecasts? For example, do you reward them if their sales forecast is within a small percentage of actual sales?
7. Do you have adequate systems in place to help you manage your sales force?

- Coordinate with marketing personnel and define the most desirable product line applications for each target account

- For each of the product lines, define the salesperson's skills necessary for the successful implementation of the product line engagement and penetration strategies

- Develop a plan for sales training using the sales kits and engagement strategies developed by marketing

- Reach consensus on the format, style, and frequency of target account reviews

- Implement a quarterly target account review process

- Use the selling cycle to forecast bookings

Operations Plan

The operations plan uses the marketing and sales plans as input. Operations normally includes engineering, production, purchasing, quality, training, and production control. The focus of operations management is on capacities, efficiencies, effectiveness, cost, quality, reliability, throughput, and customer satisfaction. This involves facilities, workflow, workplace layout, specifications, operating instructions and training. Labor, material, and overhead costs form the foundation of successful operations management.

Your operations plan should include the following areas:

- Define your manufacturing costs and separate cost for labor, material, and overhead

- Define your production capacities including product mix limitations

- Define how much additional capacity in excess of current demand you prefer to maintain, for example, +15%, or +20% for two quarters out

- Define your key performance indicators, for example, throughput time, performance against schedule, yield, customer returns, and so on

- Develop an aggressive cost-reduction plan for each product line that reflects the cost reduction needs projected by marketing

---

Checklist 11

Questions for Developing the Operations Plan

1. What is your capacity utilization by process flow? Constraints?

2. Is your facility organized for maximum flexibility and throughput?

3. Do you have adequate information systems in place to help you manage your operations efficiently and effectively?

4. How does your scrap or yield loss compare with that of your competition?

5. Is a cross training matrix in place?

6. Has your productivity been increasing or decreasing?

7. Are quality specifications written and in place? Are these specifications being followed? How do you know?

- Define your inventory and production control philosophy, for example, build to forecast, build to order, or build to stock

- Define your philosophy and stance with regard to employee selection, placement, and training

- Define how statistical quality control will help you achieve your goals

- Define how increased automation can improve your competitiveness

Research and Development Plan

Research and development (R&D) runs the gamut from a small number of people in operations looking at the next-generation production equipment to a full-time staff of professional researchers working on inventing a new family of products. Both extremes take input from the strategic marketing plan. Independent-thinking R&D staff members add their own perspective on major trends that may be emerging.

The following areas should be included in your research and development plan:

- Define a parallel approach to work on the current and next-generation products and processes

---

Checklist 12

Questions for Developing the Research and Development Plan

1. How do your R&D efforts relate to those of your competition?
2. What opportunities exist for breakthrough thinking?
3. Do you want to have a two pronged-approach; applied and basic research? How and when do they converge?
4. Do you have some R&D resources assigned to investigate the more successful of your competitors' products?
5. Do your R&D and strategic marketing people meet regularly?
6. Does your organization require R&D efforts for products or processes or both?
7. What resources are necessary to deliver a sound R&D effort?
8. Do you periodically populate engineering teams with members of the R&D group? Vice versa?
9. Are there R&D consortia in which you might participate?

- Define, as a company, your philosophy regarding technology leadership
- Define the percentage of sales you wish to earmark for R&D
- Discuss the role of R&D in human resource development
- Discuss how to give your R&D efforts visibility across your company

Human Resources Plan

Although a solid human resources plan has a tremendous amount to offer, it is often overlooked in the business planning process. A strong human resources (HR) plan can address employee selection and placement, turnover, career development, education and training, university relations, equal employment opportunities, and affirmative action. Forward-looking HR professionals can be an active force in guiding school curricula, as well as providing summer internships and other opportunities for faculty development. For high-skilled

---

> ### *Checklist 13*
> ## Questions for Developing the Human Resources Plan
>
> 1. What is your philosophy toward human resource development?
> 2. What would be the competitive advantage for your company if you were able to reduce labor costs by 25 percent?
> 3. What is your current level of turnover by major job classification, and how much does that cost your company annually?
> 4. What is your approach to training and development?
> 5. Are the goals and objectives of training linked to the goals and objectives of the business plan?
> 6. If your company recruits new college grads, what is the colleges' view of your company as a desirable place to work?
> 7. Do you have strategic alliances with forward-thinking university faculty?

industries, HR professionals can serve on industry/education steering committees and help develop the next generation employee.

Your human resources plan should include the following areas:

- HR personnel must take the initiative to understand the business in which their company is engaged
- Define an approach to reduce labor operating costs
- Apply the tools of selection and placement to improve job performance and satisfaction
- Study employee turnover and absenteeism with specific goals to reduce both
- Understand the demands your company places on its employees and chair industry group efforts to improve the fit
- Develop industry groups where non-proprietary data can be shared on compensation, turnover, selection, and placement
- Investigate the power of HR consortia to share HR R&D expenses while working on problems common to all

---

Critical Risks and Contingencies

The critical risks and contingencies section of your business plan is where you place those things that wake you in the middle of the night in a cold sweat. These are the critical risks to your business and the contingencies you know of now that can be used to combat them. If your company is in an earthquake zone, for example, you will want to plan how to deal with such a disaster. Risks can be less catastrophic, however, and may include such risks as the loss of key people. Regardless of the scope of the plan, a certain amount of comfort is obtained by reviewing the major risks that face the company.

Your critical risks and contingencies plan should include the following areas:

• Briefly evaluate the nature of the risk

• Identify contingencies that could be used to neutralize or minimize the negative consequences of the risks

• Identify specific resources that would be required to implement a contingency

• Investigate resource sharing consortia in the event of an industry-wide disaster

---

Checklist 14

Questions for Developing the Critical Risks and Contingencies Plan

1. Who are the key people on which the organization depends to achieve the goals of the business plan? How can those people be backed up?

2. What key processes or pieces of equipment run the risk of shutting your operations down if they are inoperative? How can these risks be minimized?

3. What provisions are there to cross-train key employees?

4. What do the key managers see as the critical risks to the business?

5. What risks and contingencies plans do your competitors have?

- Validate risk definition and contingency development via discussion groups
- Determine whether or not detailed implementation plans need to be developed separate from this summary

Historical and Pro Forma Financial Statements

Although the focus of your financial statements is on the present, you should include five years of historical data in the financial section. Break down the most recent three years by quarter and the oldest two by year. Include a five-year projection with the first three years by quarter and the last two by year. It is also very interesting to compute quarterly percent changes for the previous three years and compare those to the percent changes projected for the next three years. Are the measures getting better or worse?

The following areas should be included in your historical and pro forma financial section:

- Define the revenue and earnings forecasts for the company

Checklist 15

Questions for Developing Financial Statements

1. Get a copy of the proposed operating budget. Ask what procedures were used to develop the numbers. Are the figures consistent with each other? If not, why not? What opportunities are there for cost reduction?

2. Ask for a variance report and study the difference between planned and actual figures. How do you explain the difference?

3. Typically, an income statement projection will make some assumptions regarding yield and/or productivity improvements. What were those assumptions and are they still valid?

4. What were the changes in the balance sheet?

5. What are your company's critical financial ratios? How do they compare against those of your competition? Your industry averages?

- Develop pro forma income or profit and loss statements for each major product or product family
- Develop a cash flow statement together with your assumptions
- Consider developing a break-even analysis for each major product line
- Capture the assumptions made and itemize any specific objectives that must be met for your financial goals to be achieved

Supporting Materials

The supporting materials section of your business plan should contain the many notes, citations, and references to marketing research sources that you wish to preserve. It is often desirable for this section to contain just a listing of the materials that are stored elsewhere.

The main purpose of the supporting materials is to provide a record of the critical sources used in the creation of the plan. Examples include summaries of marketing research studies in which the essential points are highlighted, notes or transcripts of important meetings, or references to diskettes containing original spreadsheet analyses or databases of original research. Organize the supporting materials section to reflect the structure of the business plan itself.

All too often, the business plan is looked on as a task to be completed rather than as a process to be engaged. When this occurs, development of the effective relationships necessary for success may be left to chance. It is in the *process* of planning that the real work is accomplished. The *contents* of the plan serve to mark your progress and help you communicate your plans to organization members who did not participate in the basic planning process.

Chapter 4

Served Markets

The definition of served markets sets the stage for effective market and marketing research activities, competitive analyses, definition of needs and wants, identification of prospective target accounts, engagement strategy, marketing communications, positioning, and successful selling. Served markets must not be defined casually or as matter of convenience.

In the previous chapter, we reviewed the overall process of business planning including a brief explanation of the relationship between total markets and served markets. Served markets are a subset of the broader total market and are defined by the type of products and services offered by your company or planned to be offered by your company. Frequently, there are multiple levels involved in the definition of total and served markets.

For example, if your company is a semiconductor company that manufactures and sells static random access memory chips (SRAMs), your total market is defined as *memory* and your served market is defined as *SRAMs*. Care in defining your served markets can pay handsome competitive dividends. For example, your ability to compete effectively is enhanced when your served markets are defined in a way that permits timely and inexpensive access to valuable market research data. Knowing the availability of market data permits you to baseline your company's performance and compare it to that of your competitors.

Sources of Information

The U.S. government provides a wealth of data and is usually the best place to start your search for marketing information. For the past 35 years, the U.S. Department of Commerce has published an almanac of industry, technology and services called the *U.S. Industrial Outlook*. Most of the industries in the *Outlook* are defined according to the government's Standard Industrial Classification (SIC) system, which is widely used by researchers and analysts.

The SIC codes are hierarchical in nature. At the highest level, economic and financial activities are grouped into nine major categories: (1) agriculture, forestry, and fishing; (2) mining; (3) construction; (4) manufacturing; (5) transportation, communications and public utilities; (6) wholesale trade; (7) retail trade; (8) finance, insurance and real estate; and (9) services. These categories are indicated by the first digit of the SIC code. Each of these nine categories is further divided into *major groups* identified by the first two digits of the SIC codes. The major groups are further divided into *industry groups* and identified by the first three digits of the SIC codes. Finally, individual *industries* are identified by all four digits of the SIC codes. Other government publications extend the classification system and go to the eight or nine-digit product code level.

We will illustrate the hierarchic structure using the semiconductor example used previously. This time, we will move from the product-code level up to the top category. SRAMs are identified using an eight-digit product code of 3674-1342. SRAMs belong to a larger group of products called *MOS Memory*, identified by the seven-digit product code of 3674-134. MOS Memory, in turn, belongs to a product group called *MOS (metal oxide semiconductor)*. This product group is defined by the six-digit product code 3674-13. MOS is a part of *Digital Monolithic Integrated Circuits*, 3674-1A, which in turn is a part of *Integrated Circuits*, 3674-1. The semiconductor industry code is 3674 which, in turn, is a part of the industry group called *Electronic Components and Accessories*, defined by the three-digit code 367. The major group is *Electrical and Electronic Machinery, Equipment and Supplies* and defined by the two-digit code, 36, which in turn belongs to the top category, manufacturing. From the top down and in tabular form, we have:

Manufacturing

  36 *Electrical and Electronic Machinery, Equipment and Supplies*
    367 *Electronic Components and Accessories*
      3674 *Semiconductors and Related Devices*
        3674-1 *Integrated Circuits*
          3674-1A *Digital Integrated Circuits*
            3674-13 *MOS (metal oxide semiconductors)*
              3674-134 *MOS Memory*
                367401342 *SRAM (static random access memory)*

Knowing the structure and the codes of the various industries and product groups unlocks a wealth of data and information compiled by the government or by industry associations. Although the number of levels differ based on the category, major group, industry group, and industry selected, all codes follow the same basic structure. Once you understand the source and structure of available information, you can develop additional criteria to help you define your company's served markets. It is also possible that the markets and products you have planned do not yet exist. In this case, look for data on similar or related products.

Useful sources of information from the federal government include the following:

1. *Annual Survey of Manufacturers*

2. *Census Catalog and Guide* (listing of reports and services)

3. *Census of Manufacturers* (manufacturing information)

4. *Census of Minerals* (mining information)

5. *Numerical List of Manufactured and Mineral Products* (detailed product ID)

6. *Producer Price Index* (contains SIC data)

7. *Standard Industrial Classification Manual*

Nongovernment Sources, available at most libraries, include the following:

1. *Gale Directory of Databases*
2. *Dun's Industrial Guide, the Metalworking Directory*
3. *Encyclopedia of Associations*
4. *National Trade and Professional Associations of the United States*
5. *Standard and Poor's Register of Corporations, Directors and Executives*
6. *Thomas Register of American Manufacturers*
7. *Yearbook of Industrial Organizations*

More and more data are being provided on the Internet. If you have access to the Internet, a good place to start is the World Wide Web.

Defining Served Markets

You can begin to define your served markets by generating criteria that are to be met by the performance of your served markets. For example, criteria such as high market growth or leading edge technology products may be closely linked to who and what you are as a company, as well as what type of company you wish to become.

If your company is an existing successful company, then you may consider your served markets pretty well defined. They are, however, open to redefinition. For example, you wish to redefine your served markets because the existing markets will not produce the revenue growth you want, or they are on a downward trend, or they do not exploit your company's technology in the most profitable way.

There is no one best set of criteria for defining served markets. The criteria you select are unique to you and your company and will change over time as your company changes. Some sample criteria for defining your served markets might include overall size of the market in units or dollars, annual growth rate, unique knowledge or insight possessed by key members of your company, type of application, type of technology, unusual opportunities for strategic partnering, level of capital investment required, opportunity for export, opportunity for import, defense related, unique patents, proprietary processes, and other competitive advantages.

Other issues to consider involve whether you want to define your served markets as vertical, horizontal, or some combination of the two. Markets are usually defined vertically when a company possesses special knowledge and expertise of those markets that permit it to offer products and services designed for specific applications. Markets are usually defined horizontally when a company's products and services have wide appeal. A combination is used when marketers believe that a company can broaden its products and services by serving both vertical and horizontal markets. Vertical markets are usually defined by the type of business, such as finance, manufacturing, banking, insurance, and health care. Horizontal markets are usually defined by business process or type of application such as accounting, order entry, purchasing, desk top computing or spreadsheet software. Marketers of products and services for vertical markets use the specialized vocabulary and practices of the market segment served. Marketers of products for horizontal markets, on the other hand, use more general terms and more widely recognized and understood ways of doing things.

One way to ensure success in the marketplace is to define your company's served markets taking advantage of the strengths of both vertically and horizontally defined markets. For example, vertical market applications generally are more specific than horizontal market applications. A good strategy is to work back and forth across the two different defined markets. An example from the high-tech sector might be helpful.

The company is a Fortune 500 firm that supplies semiconductors, board products, and disk drives to computer manufacturers. Within the company, twelve strategic business units (SBUs) each had responsibility for marketing and product development for their respective markets. The more successful SBUs used their technical knowledge and expertise in each of the vertical markets to work with major customers to design and build high-performance products that enhanced their customers' position in their marketplace. Being part of the customer's design team provided a opportunity to learn more about the performance demands faced by the customer in each of their served markets. It also provided an opportunity to integrate functions into less expensive and more reliable integrated circuits rather than using a larger number of individual components. Pooling the information from all customers also enabled the company to be aware of emerging trends and to develop the next generation of products.

When seeking to define your company's served market, look first to the markets that will be served by your customers, and then work backward to define your company's served markets. Look beyond your customer base to your customer's customers to understand the products' end use. Are the products being used as they were intended or designed to be used? What do the users like and dislike about the product? What is their perception of value versus price. What do they know and how do they feel about the products' fit, form, and function? Do the data support the way your served markets are defined or do they cry out for a different definition? Listen to what the markets are saying!

Characterizing Major Needs and Wants

Once you have defined each of your served markets, it is time to build a broad matrix of needs and wants for each of your current and planned product lines. The terms *needs* and *wants* are often used interchangeably, but there is a psychological difference between the two. *Needs* convey a sense of insufficiency or dependency, while *wants* imply a desire for enhancement. Both are important when seeking to gather information about your customers, whether you sell a high-technology product to other manufacturers or process a specialty food product. Here is an example from the meat-processing industry.

Suppose you are the marketing manager of a specialty meat-processing company that supplies ground beef patties and specialty cooked meats to businesses and institutions such as hotels, schools, and restaurants. Customers are now asking you to supply a new product, specialty seasoned sliced meats. This is a new product and in some cases a new served market. Most of the people asking about the new products are in markets served by highly specialized delicatessens and most are national chains. The markets they serve are not the same, however. Each chain serves a clientele with differing tastes. A quick analysis indicates that the margins could be pretty good. How do we get an idea of the expected needs and wants of this new market?

The best thing to do is to visit several of the potential customers' sites at several different times of the day. First the customer. Who are the customers? Are they upscale? Students? Working folks? Young professionals? Neighborhood regulars? How are they dressed? How much time do they spend? What do they buy? Are they health conscious? Are the portions small, medium, or large? Do they appear concerned with the fat content of the food? Do they pay by cash, check, or credit card? Does it look like they've been there before? What are their comments about the food?

What about the Delis? Where are they located? How are they furnished? Do most of the customers eat in or take out? Are they clean? How do the customers know where to go and how to place their orders? Is the flow efficient and effective? Is the signage clear and consistent with the type of customers? How are the employees? Are they well trained? Courteous? Well groomed? What's the capacity of the Deli? What would you estimate their costs to be? What is your estimate of waste?

What about the food? What food types are people ordering the most? Is it beef? Pork? Chicken? Turkey? What types of seasonings are the most popular? What do they taste like? What are the grades of food? What are the estimated weights of each of the most popular foods? Summarize your observations under three different headings: customers, place, and food. What opportunities are there for your company to add value? For example, you might make the following observations:

- Customers:
  - Mostly 18 to 30 years old
  - Occupationally mixed, large number of students but some young professionals, not many trades people, all well-groomed and in good health
  - Most popular items are spiced meat sandwiches
  - Most comment favorably about the food and express high level of desire for full flavored meats

- Place:
  - Most delis located in areas of high foot traffic, close to universities, theaters, shopping, other fast food establishments
  - Delis furnished with small tables suitable for two, tile floor, painted walls
  - Flow a little constricted, place your order and self pick-up, pour your own drinks
  - Efficient kitchen allows for small staff
  - Limited storage
  - High inventory turns require frequent food deliveries
  - Training could be better in terms of food handling
- Food:
  - Men tend to order spiced beef and pork, women order some of the same but tend to order more smoked turkey
  - Pepper, chili, garlic, and smoked meats are most popular
  - Portions seem to average about two ounces for regular size sandwiches and three ounces for specials
  - All sandwiches are made to order
  - Commercial grades of beef and pork are used
  - Specially baked breads are used throughout

You would then reinterpret your observations in terms of needs and wants as follows:

- Needs
  - A 6- to 8-hour shelf life with limited drying, no loss of flavor, and no strong taste
  - Thin sliced cuts to enhance flavor
  - Bulk packages with variable quantities
  - Frequent deliveries with short lead-times
  - Help in sales promotion
  - Consistent quality, especially taste of seasonings
  - Low fat content
  - Attractive introductory pricing

- Wants
  - Marketing development funds for special promotions
  - Volume pricing that is consistent and aggressive
  - Long-term relationship (100 percent of business is available for the right supplier)
  - Would like some help on training staff on food handling
  - Help in improving capacity and throughput of each store
  - Computer automated ordering

From these needs and wants, you can develop a specification for a new product line—sliced meats. But before you do that, you will need a sense of who the major competitors might be.

Identifying Major Competitors

When penetrating new markets, the major competitors are the ones who have the business currently. If you don't know who they are, just ask the customers. Once you have the competitors' names, you can access the sources listed at the beginning of this chapter to help you gather more information about each of them. You can also get information on competitors from trade associations—in this example, the National Association of Meat Purveyors—of which your company is probably a member. Ask the association for the names and addresses of companies who supply the type of product you are considering—in our example, specialty meats to the delicatessen market.

Next you would identify the major competitors and develop a sense of how they might respond to your actions. What are the names of each of the major competitors? What are their histories? Which markets do they serve? What are they particularly noted for? What are their estimated shares-of-market? In which of their served markets are they the strongest? What are their strengths and assets? What are their weak points? What do you believe their actions will be in response to your new products? How can you develop your new products and services to amplify your strengths and minimize your weaknesses?

You can incorporate the answers to these questions in your specification of your new products.

Chapter 5

The Product Portfolio

Developing a product portfolio is a high-risk, never-ending activity. You never know in advance whether the products you have developed for each of your served markets will be successful. To minimize the potential for failure and maximize the probability for success, the responsibility for the development of the product portfolio should be shared primarily between the two marketing functions, strategic and tactical, with sales providing the all-important customers' perspective. Given the diversity and rate of change in the marketplace, success requires the combined resources of strategic marketing, tactical marketing, and sales. This chapter describes how to make use of the resources of all three functions in the development of a successful product portfolio.

Defining the Product Portfolio

Your portfolio of products is the means by which your company participates in each of its served markets. When your products meet the needs and wants of your served markets and your sales and service are effective, your company is successful. When they don't, it isn't.

The product portfolio is the fundamental link between strategy and tactics. Strategic marketing takes the long look ahead and works from the top down to construct the big picture. Tactical marketing converts the long-range goals into mid-range and short-range goals and develops specific products to satisfy specific markets. Dialogue and interaction between these two functions are essential.

When companies experience a delay in the introduction of new products or in the change from one product line to another, it usually indicates that the relationship between strategic marketing and tactical marketing needs work. For example, strategic marketing is responsible for the long look ahead, specifically the relationship between the longer-term strategic view of product lines, rather than the current and near-term view of product development of tactical marketing.

The dominant approach to developing your product portfolio is to first identify your served markets and then define the products that serve the needs and wants of each of those markets. On the other hand, however, there will be occasions where the combined knowledge of marketing and sales will see an opportunity for a product that presently does not exist. When this happens, a new product idea can actually create a new market. A case in point is the microprocessor and Intel Corporation.

Intel did not set out to develop the microprocessor. At the time, neither the microprocessor nor the microcomputer market existed. The company recognized the potential value of such a product only after a contract for the design of a proprietary calculator chip, commissioned by a Japanese company, fell through. Intel, seeking to salvage something from the canceled contract, negotiated for the rights to the device, redesigned it, and the first microprocessor was born. The rest is history! Breakthrough thinking of this type occurs when you blend chance occurrences with awareness and sensitivity to how the current products fit or do not fit with the current and planned markets.

Strategic Marketing

With strategic marketing charged with the responsibility for the longest look ahead, it is appropriate for strategists to set the stage by broadly defining the product lines, product groups, and product families that make up the product portfolio. The terms, *product line, product group* and *product family* refer to the different levels of product aggregation. For example, a series of specific part numbers make up a product line. A series of product lines form a product group, and various product groups form a product family.

Working backward using an example from the high-tech industry might be helpful. In the microcomputer business, notebook computers might represent the product family. Type of application might be used to define the product group within this family. For example, notebooks used in docking applications versus stand-alones may define two different product groups. Type of CPU and speed of the CPU might in turn define the product line. The schema selected for organizing and structuring your product portfolio can be useful in tracking product success in each of your served markets.

A less high-tech example involves a meat company's products. The specific product is pastrami. Pastrami is a member of the beef product line which in turn belongs to the broader product family, cooked meats.

Tactical Marketing

Once marketing strategists have defined the broad product lines, groups, and families, tactical marketing is responsible for the specific and detailed product development efforts and for the development of the market. If the dual responsibilities are working effectively, the strategic marketing team has defined the broad product lines and the resources required to produce or acquire them. The definition of these product lines includes some sense of the degree of manufacturing flexibility that might be required as tactical marketing develops specific products. This flexibility can lead to lower development costs, shorter time to market, and increased reliability of new products.

In the microelectronics business, for example, time to market is a critical factor in a company's ability to compete effectively. If the broad product lines are too narrowly defined by marketing strategists, then the tactical marketing group has less design flexibility as they seek to satisfy current market needs. When this occurs, new product development activities take too long, cost too much, and the window of opportunity is missed. How can you avoid this? The best way is through constant dialogue between the two groups: What is selling well? What is not selling well? Do we know why?

Features and Benefits

One of most difficult areas in the product portfolio development is deciding on the feature set for each of the products. If too many features are chosen, you not only confuse your customers but also add to the time and development cost of the product. If too few features are chosen, your customers feel product value is lacking. A general guide is to confirm that new product features meet the needs of customers. Sage advice is often found in the phrase, "less is more."

Once the customers' basic needs are addressed, you can vary the product features to address the customers' wants. The key is to get your new products to market as quickly as possible with the set of features that best satisfies customers' basic needs. Once again, to maximize the probability of success, remember the importance of constant dialogue between strategic marketing, tactical marketing, and sales.

Linking Needs and Wants to Features and Benefits

An area of vulnerability for manufacturers and marketers of high-tech products is their tendency to focus on the features of the product rather than on the benefits. Marketing people in high-tech companies may be trained engineers first and marketers second. As engineers, they spend most of their time developing and refining technically sophisticated products and less time developing the processes by which their products are marketed, sold, and serviced. They often believe that the buying decision is a rational process, and if they present the features of their products clearly, the customer will make the right decision. Most high-tech companies interact with their marketplace with a method that they have been using for years: seminars, trade shows, and print media.

Communications and Positioning

To get the word out about their products and services, high-tech companies host technical seminars, participate in trade shows, and advertise in trade magazines. These outlets emphasize the technical features of the company's latest products and tend to read like an abbreviated specification. The goal of this type of advertising is to generate sales leads which are then followed up by the sales force. It doesn't always happen!

Seminars, Trade Shows, and Print Media

The vehicle used most commonly for these sales leads are "bingo" cards. These *reader service cards* are postcard-size requests for more information. In the case of seminars, they are distributed to the attendees. In the case of magazines, they are included in the issue. They are used to request a reprint of an article or to request additional information about your company, your products, or your services. It is scary, but this may be the primary interface between your company and your prospective customers!

The bingo cards contain some qualifying information that the reader fills out at the time of the request. This is usually limited to the type of business in which the company is engaged, organization function, number of employees, and buying plans for the future. When the cards are mailed, they are usually routed to a third-party literature fulfillment house where, several weeks later, the requested information is sent to the requester. The literature fulfillment house may also be under contract to the company to qualify the leads further and forward them to the company's sales organization. Qualification, at this level, usually consists of a telemarketing person calling the requester and asking some questions about their title, job responsibility, decision-making authority, budget level, planned application, and projected timeline—all good information but starting to get a little cold by now.

The qualified leads are then delivered by U.S. mail to the company's sales department. It's not uncommon for these leads (which are now several weeks old) to languish in someone's in-basket until they determine that a large enough number has accumulated to warrant packing them up and shipping them, once again via U.S. mail, to the responsible sales manager. The sales manager is then expected to distribute the leads to the appropriate sales person for action. What's wrong with this picture?

To begin with, the sales manager usually doesn't know, in advance, that the leads are coming and, when they arrive, usually has no idea of what ad generated them or when they were generated. Besides that, anywhere from several weeks to several months may have elapsed since the original request was made, and no self-respecting salesperson wants to do such a follow-up. As a consequence, the leads are usually not acted upon! Now, we will speculate how the process can be improved using the account development cycle as a model and current information technology.

Marketing and Sales On-Line

First, you have to have some basic hardware and software capability. We recommend that you provide your marketing and salespeople with notebook or laptop computers equipped with high-speed modems (28.8 Kbps minimum) and loaded with standard software packages such as Microsoft Office or Lotus SmartSuite. Include a software product such as LapLink to enable the users to synchronize their desktop files with their notebook files as well as to provide simple remote file sharing resources. Simple contact management capability exists within Office and SmartSuite or, even better, use Lotus Notes. Notes is a powerful flexible groupware product that will grow with your company.

Strategic Marketing. Using the relational model, marketing strategists take the lead in overall business planning and define the markets to be served and the products for each. Review each of your served markets and your product portfolio and understand how the buying decisions are made for each market and product. Review your marketing communications or positioning strategy and verify that the information channels selected are valid. This includes conducting any required marketing research. Make this information available on your network. Pattern the structure of your information after some of the better Web Pages on the Internet.

Marketing strategists prepare and publish the long-term forecast, based on the historical growth rates of the served markets plus projected share-of-market goals. The tactical marketing group and operations managers then use this initial forecast by market segment and product line for subsequent planning. The marketing strategists post and maintain the forecast on the network for free access by the tactical marketing group as they take on the task of market development. Tactical marketing in turn prepares a short-term operating forecast which becomes the basis for the monthly, quarterly, and annual revenue forecast. Typically, the short-term forecast is updated monthly and the long-term forecast is updated semi-annually. These marketing forecasts serve as the planning basis for the business. Posting the forecast to the network also eliminates costly time delays and unnecessary work when it is updated.

Tactical Marketing. Marketing strategists are responsible for the definition of served markets and the definition of broad product lines. The tactical marketing group is responsible for market development and the development of specific products. As tactical marketing professionals are responsible for specific product development, they are the ones most qualified to identify prospective buyers or target accounts using the many electronic databases available. A number of commercial data bases can be accessed on-line. Marketing tacticians can quickly screen tens of thousands of companies to produce a short list of prospective accounts, by sales territory, saving much time and money. Tactical marketers can then use their knowledge of the prospective accounts, and the probability of certain product applications emerging within the accounts, to construct a sales kit and an engagement strategy for use by the sales force.

The sales kit is the crown jewel of the relational process and contains all the information the salesperson needs when calling on, qualifying, and developing the account. The sales kit is all-electronic, and its contents are distributed electronically. Using standard presentation software as that in Office or SmartSuite, tactical marketers can craft and assemble multiple presentations to support the different types of sales presentations. Sample spreadsheets can be embedded in the kit and photographs scanned in. The multiple presentations provide the salespeople with a consistent message whether they are presenting to senior management or to procurement yet, at the same time, presents the information in a way that is consistent with the customer's knowledge and experience. For example, when presenting to senior management, salespeople will emphasize those factors that are important to management. These are typically not the same factors that are important to engineers. The messages are consistent, however, at all levels of the organization.

Marketing can also use the sales kit in training the sales force. The sales kit contains copies of related articles, white papers, product data sheets, testimonials, and competitive profiles. The kits are posted to the network and are downloaded by the salespeople as needed. With prospective customers defined, sales kits constructed, and engagement strategies defined, the "shotgun" approach to advertising can be replaced with narrowly focused efforts. All information can be distributed electronically in a very short time. As changes are made to the sales kit, LapLink or similar software allows your salespeople to download only those portions of the sales kit that have changed.

Sales. Salespeople are highly skilled individuals with limited time and resources. They are expert in calling on customers, developing relationships, and using those relationships to help them identify, qualify, develop, and close sales opportunities. Unfortunately, they are often given tasks that decrease their face-to-face selling time and contribute nonproductively to their workloads. To help lighten their load and increase available selling time, do not ask them to prospect or to forecast demand for their territory. This is a waste of their time.

What is important, within the account development model, is for the salespeople to use the short list of prospective accounts to identify and track each of the emerging opportunities through their respective selling cycles. These efforts produce the rich data required by marketers to gauge the success of their strategy and tactics. With the data available electronically on the network, individual users can structure and review the information in any manner they desire. For example, marketing strategists might be interested in a top-down analysis by market segment and major product line. Marketing tacticians, on the other hand, might be interested in a bottom-up analysis of individual products by specific customer. With the basic data available electronically, the salesperson does not have to spend extra time putting analyses together to satisfy the requests of different people. Each user can access the data and generate analyses specific to his or her needs. As each salesperson tracks opportunities, using suitable software, he or she develops a complete account history that can then be accessed for regularly scheduled account reviews.

The purpose of the account review is to conduct a business won/business lost analysis to verify that strategic assumptions and tactical plans are still on track. Detailed account reviews should be held quarterly and be attended by representatives of strategic marketing, tactical marketing, and sales. Sales management chairs the meetings. Each salesperson is asked to review each of his or her accounts. The reviews are used to help manage the business and validate the assumption and effectiveness of the sales kits, training, and engagement strategy. Are we on-track or off-track? Do we know why we're winning or why we're losing the business?

It's important to spend a few minutes to describe the process. Hard copies are not made. With notebook computers and an LCD projection panel, each salesperson can use their notebook computers to step through each of their accounts. With the salesperson tracking each opportunity through its respective sales cycle, there is no additional time required to prepare for the account reviews. All information is readily available!

Chapter 6

Market Segmentation

Market segmentation is the subdivision of served markets in a manner that enhances the company's competitive position. Unlike many marketers and marketing researchers, we do not use *segmentation* synonymously with *market definition*. In consumer marketing, for example, segmentation is used to categorize consumers into subgroups or clusters based on common characteristics, such as buying power, age, geographic location, or lifestyle. Consumer marketers believe that these subgroups facilitate advertising. It is interesting to note, however, that as our use of computer technology increases, the size of these subgroups approaches one! That is a trend that should not be ignored.

In business-to-business marketing, most of the companies that offer products and services requiring a complex sale usually have not segmented their markets beyond their served markets. Segmentation, however, can subdivide those served markets into segments that can be used to exploit competitive strengths. The definition of served markets should be guided largely by the type and level of comparative data that are available.

Segmentation Criteria

Served markets can be segmented using criteria similar to those used by consumer marketing, or criteria unique to your company and your products can be developed. A good way is to construct a served market by product line matrix and use that to determine your segmentation criteria. The goal of any such segmentation is to divide the population of prospective target accounts into smaller groups with special interests, affinities, characteristics, or attributes.

For example, if your company designs, develops, and markets microcomputer software for publishing companies, your served market is publishing. Based on your existing product lines you could segment your served market into graphic design, CAD/CAM, and productivity tools. These three segments would then constitute your served market. Other companies may or may not segment their served markets the same way. Your major competitors are likely to segment their served market in a similar way, but it may not be identical. A company may be a major competitor in one segment but offer no competitive products in the other segments. How companies segment their markets often is a clue to how they view the broader markets.

Sample Criteria

When segmenting your served markets, it is helpful to look first at your customers and then at their customers and then at their customers until you reach the end user. Match the data about the end user against the data about your served market. Look at each level of the product chain considering the following factors:

- Type of application
- Application itself
- Performance: speed, capacity, color, and so on
- Price points
- Standard, custom, or semicustom products
- Physical size of product
- Quality of product
- Reliability of product
- Packaging of product
- Service
- Relationship with other products

The type of segments selected can mean the difference between leadership and mediocrity. The creative edge falls to the marketers who see, challenge, and take advantage of what others take for granted. Once the market segments have been defined, the next step is to identify the unit and dollar size of each of the defined segments.

TAM, SAM, and SOM

The terms *TAM, SAM* and *SOM* are defined in Chapter 3 (strategic planning). Briefly, *TAM* means "Total Available Market" and relates to the size of the broader market of which your segmented markets are a part. Size is defined in units and dollars and includes all products that comprise the market whether made by your company or not. The dollars are almost always given in current dollars, so year-to-year growth comparisons, to be accurate, must be adjusted for inflation.

SAM means "Served Available Market" and is defined as that portion of the total market that is served by your company's products. Its size can never be any larger than the TAM. It is also defined in units and dollars. SAM dollars are almost always given in current dollars, as well, and therefore will require adjustment when comparing year-to-year growth.

SOM means "Share of Market" and is determined by your company's actual sales. Share of market is a key concept, and, therefore, it is important to understand how it is computed. SOM relates to your company's SAM. If you compute SOM based on the total market (TAM) and your served market is a smaller portion of the total market, you are significantly understating your market share. SOM percentages should be computed for both units and dollars, so you can compare your company's sales price against the average sales prices. These and other types of analyses can be very helpful in guiding marketing and sales efforts.

Analyses

It is important to look at TAM, SAM, and SOM as an interrelated system. If your company's goals are to grow at a certain compounded rate, say 10 to 12 percent per year, then it is important to understand the rates at which your TAM, SAM, and SOM are projected to grow and how those growth rates influence your product portfolio and your projected margins. For example, if the TAM is growing at a rate greater than your target rate but your SAM is not, you know that you will have to serve a broader piece of the market to increase SAM. If your SAM is growing at the desired rate, you know that you can maintain a given SOM and still make your revenue goals. On the other hand, if your SAM is not growing at the desired rate, then to achieve your revenue goals you must increase your share of market.

To increase your share of market means that you must take market share away from your competitors. Knowing and understanding the markets' growth rates can help you formulate your plans and help you understand the strategy that is most likely to be followed by your major competitors. This type of information is also important in formulating the profitability goals for each of your product lines.

Establishing Profitability Goals

To be most effective, profitability goals must be established for each of the major product lines and the specific segments they serve. It is best to pursue a product-line profitability model right from the start. This may cause some concern on the part of your finance people, however, especially if their cost accounting systems can't break down costs as needed.

Begin with the revenue projections for the corporation (Chapter 3, "Strategic Planning"). If not done previously, break the corporate revenue and margin projections down into their respective product-line groupings. Compute the gross and net margins for each current and planned product line. How do current versus planned product margins compare? With few exceptions, our experience is that the actual current margins are usually less than the planned margins. It is therefore important to discuss the two major philosophical approaches to margin planning. One approach, called *outside-in* looks first at the level of sales price that is likely to be supported in the market to achieve a given level of penetration or share of market. From the sales price, the desired margin is subtracted and the underlying costs defined. The other approach, called *inside-out*, begins with the cost, which is marked up to yield the sales price. The outside-in approach is preferred because share of market, sales price, cost, and margin are all linked dynamically.

Developing Price, Distribution, and Promotion Strategies

For your market segmentation strategies to be successful, you must also look at product line strategies for price, distribution, and promotion. Like marketing and sales, price, distribution, and promotion are interdependent. For example, price and market share influence the sales channels through which you distribute your products, and the sales channels influence your margins at a given price. Different distribution channels carry different cost structures and require different types of advertising and market communications to be successful. For example, products can be distributed through manufacturer's representatives, resellers, distributors, or handled by a direct sales force. Each of these distribution channels has benefits and drawbacks and, in crafting your segmentation strategy, each must be considered. Constructing a matrix as shown in Exhibit 6.1 is often helpful.

Price

Products priced the same will not yield identical margins across the different distribution channels. The different distribution channels vary in costs for advertising, flooring, stock rotation, market development, and price protection. These additional costs, if unrecognized, can contribute to product margins being much lower than planned. The best advice is to look at the distribution needs of your market and then develop specific pricing strategies for each.

Distribution

Each distribution channel has its own benefits and drawbacks. A direct sales force offers stability, continuity, loyalty, product knowledge, orga-

Product Lines/Segments:	Consumer	Corporate	Education
Notebook	X	X	–
Desktop	X	X	–
Server	–	X	X
Introductory Price Points:			
Notebook	$1595	$2195	–
Desktop	$2295	$2795	$1795
Server	–	$3495	$2195
Distribution Channel:			
Notebook	Special Mailer (1)	Reseller	–
Desktop	Mail Order (2)	Reseller	Direct
Server	–	Reseller	Direct
Promotion Strategies:			
Notebook	Joint Promo	Special MDF (3)	–
Desktop	Discount	Special MDF	Sales Calls (4)
Server	–	Special MDF	Sales Calls
Expected Gross Margins (%):			
Notebook	35	23	–
Desktop	30	23	20
Server		28	25

Notes:
1. Special mailer involves joint mail/marketing campaign with a major credit card company. They provide a once a year mailing to their special customers as a service. Highest expected margin due to prequalified customers.
2. Regular mail order discounting costs us 5 percentage points on expected margin.
3. Requires $500K discretionary market development funds (MDF) for reseller. Price protection and inventory rotation allowances also lower expected margins.
4. No special promotion planned.

Exhibit 6.1

Price, Distribution, and Promotion Matrix

nizational knowledge, and a direct link to the factory. Direct sales is also very desirable when your product lines are complex, narrowly focused, highly technical, and require continuous dialogue with the marketing people. The negative aspect of direct sales is that it may take longer to train and develop direct sales personnel, plus, at low sales volume, direct sales is expensive.

Manufacturer's representatives offer short start-up time, competence, relationships with the customers in their territories, and a self-managing sales function. Reps are used widely in the high-tech marketplace and are usually heavily staffed with engineers. This means that they can understand complex technical products quickly, but it does not mean that they know how to sell them. Using the account development model described in this book, with the sales kits and the engagement strategy defined by marketing, this approach may work well for you. Another advantage of using manufacturer's representatives is that reps are usually paid a fixed percentage, based on the revenue they generate, so selling costs are known.

Resellers are firms that agree to purchase a certain minimum volume of product from the manufacturer and, in turn, resell it into specially segmented markets using their own direct sales force. The computer industry makes wide use of value-added resellers who offer services to the customer beyond those offered by the manufacturer. Examples of these services include 24-hour service, spare parts maintenance, training, cabling, networking, and software sales. In other industries, such services include stock management, and display and promotion support (such as co-op advertising). Resellers can help develop markets, but cost can become a problem. Many ask for special price protection, stock rotation, flooring, and market development funds.

Distributors come in all shapes and sizes, from small specialty distributors who have built their reputations as trusted suppliers to the major suppliers. Distributors also have their own sales force, work on fairly thin margins, and depend on high turnover to make their profits. Most require that the manufacturer maintain ownership of the inventory that is in their facility. Distributors also differentiate themselves by adding special services such as testing, marking, and special packaging. They also ask for price protection, stock rotation, and special deals.

Promotion

Promotional efforts can be enhanced if marketers develop strategies specific to each of the distribution channels. We know from our previous discussion that different channels serve differing needs of the marketplace. For example, high-tech products require a complex sale. We also know that different organization levels are involved in the buying decision. Engineers look at things differently than middle managers, who look at things differently than executives. Each segment of the buying population reads different magazines. So your promotional strategies ought to take these differences into consideration. For the executive who reads *Business Week*, for example, emphasize ease of use and less network delays rather than integrated circuits and high bandwidth.

Construct the sales kit in such a way to make maximum use of specific promotional strategies. Using standard presentation software, assemble multiple slide presentations to support the different buying needs of the various levels of the organization. Scan reprints of ads into the presentations to amplify ad recognition. Embed sample spreadsheets and product photographs if appropriate. The messages will then be consistent at all levels of the organization. Because the sales kit is distributed electronically, special promotional efforts can be on every salesperson's desktop computer the next day.

Part III

Tactical Marketing

Chapter 7

The Role, Responsibilities and Relationships of Tactical Marketing

The perspective of tactical marketing differs slightly from that of strategic marketing. While marketing strategists are responsible for the definition of the product lines and the markets to be served, marketing tacticians are responsible for converting those plans into shippable product that satisfies the customers' needs and wants at a price and quality that are satisfactory to both the customers and the company.

The Role of Tactical Marketing

Broadly speaking, the primary role of tactical marketing is to refine product lines that were defined initially by marketing strategists, develop specific products, and bring them to market in a cost-effective manner. This means tweaking product features to modify fit, form, and function and adjusting planned price, cost and volume requirements to meet the needs and wants of the current and near-term markets. Tactical marketing may also be known as product management or product line management. It is a key function that requires continuous dialogue with sales and strategic marketing to be effective.

Major Responsibilities

Working within the categories of planned product lines and the capabilities of current and future technologies, marketing tacticians identify the needs and wants of the served markets and develop specific products for each of the served market segments defined. This check-and-balance function serves two purposes. First, it verifies or refutes the accuracy and foresight of the earlier efforts of marketing strategists. Second, it builds maximum flexibility into the organization's ability to respond to the changing needs and wants of the marketplace. This flexibility and shared responsibility also helps prevent product marketing from becoming overly invested in a specific product design that may no longer be suitable.

Marketing tacticians build upon marketing strategists' earlier research to reaffirm or redefine the performance, price, and cost parameters for their products. This includes conducting any additional market and marketing research that may be required, as well as test marketing. They also provide feedback to marketing strategists regarding their findings. Marketing strategists use this feedback to update their position on the next generation of product line migration plans.

Another key responsibility of marketing tacticians is to define, for each product line, the prospective target accounts and the projected product applications within each of the accounts. This involves understanding the business in which each prospective account is engaged and the markets they serve. Together with the sales organization, marketing tacticians also define the selling cycle for each product line and establish introductory and subsequent pricing needed to meet or exceed the planned volume, share-of-market, and profitability goals established by marketing strategists. Any differences between strategic and tactical marketing plans are reconciled before proceeding.

Marketing tacticians are also responsible for constructing the sales kit, providing new product training to the sales force, and establishing the engagement strategy. The sales kit contains a summary of the needs and wants of the prospective accounts embedded in a series of slide or overhead presentations constructed with standard presentation software. The sales kit also contains product data sheets and sales support documentation that fits with how the prospective accounts go about their decision-making process. This includes a summary table of the features and benefits of the company's products compared with those of major competitors.

When marketing tacticians use their knowledge of the products and of the target market and generate a short list of prospective accounts with suggested application ideas, the salespeople no longer have to prospect their territories to locate the most likely customers. Eliminating this prospecting task allows the field salesperson to increase face-to-face selling time by about 20 percent! Marketing tacticians also assume responsibility for the revenue forecast; but more on that later.

Relationship to Strategic Marketing and Sales

Tactical marketing has a direct relationship with strategic marketing and sales and an indirect relationship with customers. Its relationships with the second and third functions is pivotal. With marketing strategists, marketing tacticians exchange information about any refinements to previously planned products and provide feedback on planned versus actual penetration, acceptability of the pricing structure adopted, plan versus actual share-of-market attained, and updates on the activities of major competitors.

Tactical marketing's relationship with sales is more hands-on and involves product training, technical support, and assistance in engaging prospective accounts. Also, the primary marketing interface for salespeople is the tactical marketing group, which is an information source and their partner in the factory. It is the responsibility of marketing tacticians, not salespeople, to present the company's future products and product migration plans; the reasons for this are explored in Chapter 11. Salespeople "own" the accounts, so it is their responsibility to arrange and schedule meetings for these future product presentations and to identify who is to attend from the customer's company, set the agenda, open and close the meetings, and initiate follow-up.

Scope

The scope of tactical marketing describes the level of product detail and the time period covered in planning and forecasting activities. Marketing tacticians plan and forecast product families and product lines. They are knowledgeable about and monitor specific product configurations but do not plan or forecast at the part-number level.

All planning and forecasting activities involve both units and dollars. When the forecast is generated in units, it can be used by operations managers for capacity planning. Marketing tacticians are also responsible for planning and forecasting their product lines' elasticity in each of their served markets, the needs of replacement markets and the saturation levels in those markets. They also should have a sense of what the competition might be expected to do in response to the company's actions.

Planning Level and Horizon

The planning horizon for tactical marketing must be long enough to allow for the successful development of the products and their positioning in the marketplace and yet be short enough to maintain a focus on revenue and profit generation. Plans should accommodate at least two generations of the product to maintain continuity in the marketplace. For products that have a life of six months or less, a planning horizon of two years is appropriate. This means that marketing tacticians are *primarily* responsible for revenue, capacity utilization, share-of-market, and profitability for two years in this case.

For example, using the example of microcomputers mentioned previously, marketing tacticians are interested in forecasting demand that is driven by their share of market assumptions rather than unit demand generated by the sales force. Tactical marketing must know the probable demand so the factory can install adequate capacity. The tactical marketing forecast is at a high level of aggregation, for example, product line or product family and is useful for capacity planning, revenue projections, and profitability forecasts. It is also extremely valuable in forecasting conversion from one product family to another.

Forecast Level and Horizon

Within the context of the relational model, marketing tacticians are responsible for the revenue forecast for their respective product families and product lines. Using the term *revenue forecast* rather than *sales forecast* avoids confusion with a sales forecast generated by the sales organization. It can save a lot of time and eliminate a lot of confusion when there is only one revenue forecast and that forecast is generated by marketing tacticians, not the sales organization. What the sales organization should forecast is described later.

The revenue forecast should be in units and dollars by product line by month, span a two-year horizon, and be updated quarterly. Some companies may publish the unit and dollar forecast in separate reports. If you do this, label them prominently to prevent confusion. Think and

Quarterly Forecast by Product Line (Notebook)								
Product Line/ Period (000s)	Q1'96	Q2'96	Q3'96	Q4'96	Q1'97	Q2'97	Q3'97	Q4'97
Notebook 486	15	13	10	5	–	–	–	–
Notebook Pentium	5	15	25	35	35	35	30	30
Notebook Pentium (Pro)	–	–	5	10	15	25	35	45
Totals	20	28	40	50	50	60	65	75
Actuals	19							
Forecast/Actual (%)	105							

Exhibit 7.1

Forecast Showing Conversion to Newer Models

work in units and then bring the units and dollars together in the profit and loss statement or in a summary report.

Monthly, as actual revenue is reported, enter the actual data and compute the monthly forecast accuracy. Once the quarterly actuals are in, compute the quarterly accuracy and update the forecast. See Exhibit 7.1 for an example of a quarterly tactical marketing forecast. The horizon then becomes a two-year rolling forecast. This two-year detailed forecast by month, coupled with the strategic marketing group's five- and ten-year forecast, gives adequate time for capacity planning. The same format can be used for the monthly forecast.

Impact of Information

Of the three functions, the information generated by tactical marketing directly impacts the near-term health and vitality of your company. This information drives the construction of annual budgets, staffing levels, capacity planning and capital equipment purchases. Tactical marketing defines near-term revenue and profitability. If effective relationships are not in place between marketing tacticians and marketing strategists, then marketing tacticians may be surprised in terms of the direction of the product lines and may find themselves playing catch-up as they seek to serve a market that won't wait. When effective relationships are in place, unexpected changes in the marketplace or aggressive acts by the competition are anticipated and dealt with accordingly. When effective relationships are in place between marketing tacticians and salespeople, there is a smooth exchange of product information and marketing's identification of the various prospective accounts and the establishment of a strategy for engagement greatly facilitates the sales organization's development of the accounts.

Chapter 8

Market Development

Market development builds on market segmentation and defined markets. Fundamental to the relational model and the account development cycle is the notion of target marketing. Each market segment served has potential applications for your company's products and services. Understanding the makeup of those applications with how your product lines can satisfy them, is a strong step forward in effective market development.

Suppose, for example, that early strategic marketing planning efforts concluded that your served markets are planned to grow, over the next five to seven years, at a 15 percent rate annually. They also indicated that the majority of applications can be grouped into five broad categories: initial capability, improved business processes, cost savings, networking, and equipment upgrades or replacements. The application matrix is used to map candidate product lines to application category within each segment served (Exhibit 8.1). Chapter 9 shows how to extend this type of thinking to the identification of prospective target accounts.

Marketing tacticians can develop additional criteria for each of the application categories. The criteria will differ depending on the market segments served. For example, not all law firms will have the same requirements for notebook computers to improve their business practices. To maximize the chances for success, the marketing tactician must understand the details of the market segments served. To do so requires ready access to extensive information. This information may be in the form of research reports commissioned by your company or may be accessed from an on-line database.

Sources of Information

Much of the information needed on product applications is available in the reference section of your local public or university library. Sometimes it is available only in print form—in large books or loose-leaf binders—but most of the time it is available in CD-ROM or on-line.

The most widely recognized information sources include names such as Dow Jones News/Retrieval Service, Mead Data Central's Nexis, Dialog, ABI/Inform, BRS/Search, and ProQuest. If you wish to use a single service, perhaps the best source available is Predicasts, offered by Information Access Company. Predicasts consists of several databases that are available in the Predicasts Terminal System (PTS). The advantage of using a single source is that you and your colleagues can become familiar with the structure of the databases and skilled in the use of search algorithms. The following databases are available in PTS:

- A/DM&T (Aerospace/Defense Markets & Technology)

- ARA (Annual Reports Abstract)

- F&S (Field and Search) Index

- Forecasts

- Infomat International Business

- MARS (Marketing & Advertising Reference Service)

- NPA/Plus (New Product Announcements/Plus)

- Newsletter Database

- PROMT (Predicasts Overview of Markets & Technology)

- Time Series

PTS offers past history, present activities, and forecasts of future markets, products, and companies. New products and technologies can be tracked and market size and market share determined. For example, hierarchical product codes are based on a modified and expanded version of the Standard Industrial Classification (SIC) codes.

Specific Databases

If you have a sufficient budget, you may be able to afford to purchase extensive information on-line. Predicasts offers a complete user's manual and in-depth training on how to access and search the various databases. Following is a brief review of each of the databases offered.

Aerospace/Defense Markets and Technologies (A/DM&T) provides access to the world's aerospace and defense literature and provides detailed information on companies, markets, and technologies. It also provides a rich array of information on defense contracts including: source, contract amount, contract number, and any special features sought. This database also covers industries that have significant defense sector business such as chemicals, electronics, computers, metals, plastics, and telecommunications. More than 30,000 new abstracts are added each year.

Annual Reports (ARA) contains information from several thousand U.S. and international companies whose stock is traded on U.S. stock exchanges. This database includes rapid growth industries such as advertising, aerospace, chemicals, communications and publishing, consumer goods, electrical equipment, electronic components, food products, personal care products, materials, pharmaceuticals, and test equipment. The emphasis is on textual material covering historical performance, current activities, and strategies at the product line level. This is an excellent source for conducting research on current markets and market conditions. ARA provides information on a wide range of business activities such as:

- Overall company performance
- Corporate structure
- Mergers, acquisitions, and joint ventures
- Product line revenues
- New products and markets
- Research and development
- Plant and facility expansions
- Marketing strategies
- Corporate and industry outlooks

Field and Search (F&S Index) provides a source citation and a one- or two-line abstract of the article identified. The database focuses on industries, products, and companies and emphasizes financials, demographics, and socioeconomic activities. The data are from about 2,000 international trade and business publications. The Index covers a broad range of manufacturing, service, and wholesale/retail trade industries.

Short-term and long-term forecasts of production, sales, and exports for all manner of business, industry, economic, and product areas are contained in the *Forecasts* database. This database is good for establishing market sizes and identifying areas that meet or exceed a specific growth rate. It covers the products and services of all major industries. More than 120,000 records are added to the database each year.

Information on industry trends, technologies, companies, and products on an international basis with a special emphasis on European business sources is contained in *Infomat*. More than 425 publications are abstracted including about 100 daily newspapers from the major business centers of the world. Non-English sources are abstracted in English. This database can be used to track competitors on a worldwide basis and can help identify market size and market share on a country-by-country basis.

Marketing and Advertising Reference Service (MARS) covers the consumer products and services industries. MARS is also a key source of information on advertising campaigns, marketing strategies, market size, market share, and advertising trends. This database can be very helpful in monitoring product positioning and the effectiveness of marketing communications as MARS contains the key Advertising/ Marketing Concept Codes defining the types of marketing and advertising. These codes enhance retrieval efforts. More than 40,000 abstracts are added each year.

The full text of several hundred industry newsletters is contained in the *Newsletter Database*. This database provides access to narrowly available information written by industry specialists and dealing with specific company activities, technological developments, and industry trends. It is international in scope and provides search capability by industry codes.

New Product Announcements/Plus (NPA/Plus) contains the full text of news releases that announce new products, modifications, new technologies, and processes. These news releases are a valuable source of information about prices, models, performance specs, distribution channels, and markets. With more than 30,000 records added annually, this becomes a great source for research on major competitors. Specific topics are covered such as:

- New products and technologies
- Product specifications, modifications, and applications
- Contracts, sales, and license agreements
- Trade names, prices, and availability
- Target markets and marketing campaigns
- Distribution channels
- Company contact names and telephone numbers
- New facilities and expansions
- Corporate financial results
- Litigation

Predicasts Overview of Markets and Technology (PROMT) covers a broad range of business and industry and is the starting point for a variety of on-line searches. You can research a product, its markets, the materials and processes used to produce it, the companies that manufacture it, and the major competitors. More than 400,000 records are added each year. Various investment analysts' reports are included.

Historical statistical records covering all aspects of the economy, demographics, industry, finance, and other business activities are found in *Time Series*. Unique indexing allows you to extract records that meet certain criteria such as unit of measure, growth rate, and data years.

These databases provide an incredible advantage to marketing tacticians as they develop their markets. The databases surveyed above can provide answers to virtually all of the questions asked in market development. Also, once the information has been located, it can be quickly and inexpensively updated as needed. Organizing this key information into an application matrix, as described in the following section, is also very helpful in forming marketing development plans.

The Application Matrix

The application matrix is simply a convenient way of showing the relationship between your company's products with their planned applications and the market segments served. Generating such a matrix or spreadsheet helps you to review the served market segments and planned applications by product line. An example from the high-tech sector will help make the matrix concept a little more concrete. Consider the following hypothetical example:

- The company is a microcomputer manufacturer
- Major product lines are server, desktop, notebook, and laptop computers
- Major markets served are manufacturing, banking, legal, healthcare, government, education, and hospitality (hotel)

Product Line: LA	Served Market: Legal			
Application	**Partner**	**Attorney**	**Paralegal**	**Office Staff**
Initial Capability	↑	↑	↑	Models a, b, c
Correspondence				↑
Client Billing				Models d, e, f
Contracts				↑
Research				
Networking	Models j, k, l	Models m, n, o	Models g, h, i	Model g, h, i

Exhibit 8.1

Sample Application Matrix

- Served markets are segmented. For manufacturing, they are segmented functionally into marketing, sales, engineering, finance, and production. For legal, they are segmented by type of professional, for example, partner, attorney, paralegal, and staff.
- Product lines support each segment
- Product applications are planned for each segment

Exhibit 8.1 shows how the application matrix looks with fictitious data. The matrix displays sample data for the LA product line and the Legal served market, which is segmented by job title. The applications include initial capability, correspondence, client billing, contracts, research, and full networking capabilities. The arrows indicate that the models listed will satisfy the market segment for all included applications. For example, the partners' models j, k, and l provide full capability to satisfy partners' needs, while the staff's initial capability models a, b, and c provide a minimum of functions to satisfy some staff needs.

Once the application matrix is constructed, it can be modified to include any number of refinements, such as scheduled introduction dates and expected competitive responses. The matrix can serve as a valuable planning tool for product positioning and marketing communications.

Product Positioning

One of the most important factors in product positioning is knowing and understanding your customers' calendars. If you sell directly to other companies, one of the first things to consider is their fiscal year, capital appropriations cycle, and their own product development schedules. This often requires you to understand *their* customers' calendars as well. Knowing the critical dates in the markets served by your customers allows you to work backward to develop plans for the qualification of your products.

Another key point to consider is your customers' internal procedures. Most larger companies have procurement standards that help them standardize the procurement of products from two or more suppliers. In some companies, the qualified list of suppliers is known as an AVL (approved vendor list). Such a list is useful when products must be compatible across different departments. Once your company's products are approved, people within individual departments can purchase them knowing that they will be compatible. These procedures must be taken into consideration in both product marketing and product positioning and marketing communication activities.

Another factor to consider is a possible shift in buying patterns. For example, early in their history, notebook and laptop computers were sold mostly to professionals in highly technical fields and to other early technology adopters. Today, most computer manufacturers note a shift in buying patterns as computers are sold either directly or indirectly to the household consumer. This is a different selling cycle and a different sales channel. In this sales channel, it is important to understand the retailers' customer calendars. Where do they buy? When do they buy? How do they buy? When are new models introduced? How are they introduced?

Although there may be some regional differences, most customer calendars are more or less consistent across retailers. Major department stores are probably the best source for information of this type. The answers to these questions can help guide your thinking in the planning and execution of specific product positioning activities.

Specific Positioning Activities

Planners of specific positioning activities draw information from the previous work on needs and wants matched with the product lines' features and benefits. This is a reiterative process in which the first step is to generate a series of candidate messages that highlight the benefits of the products. At this point, it is helpful to relate the benefits to the features so you can keep track of the connection between the two.

It is best to plan positioning activities in concert with the marketing communications people. They are expert in generating the words, phrases, and graphics that communicate the most important messages about your company and your products clearly and succinctly. They are also knowledgeable about the effectiveness of different media and the costs associated with each. These skills make them important members of your marketing team.

Marketing Communications

A complex sale often involves technologies and concepts that are new to the customer and invariably, whether the technologies and concepts are familiar or not, includes multiple groups of people and several different decision makers in the buying decision. These different groups and decision makers frequently have differing needs and wants and often go about their decision making in very different ways. For example, sales and accounting, engineering and customer service may have very different requirements. Because of these differences, a complex sale usually requires several different sales presentations to different levels of the organization before the sale is closed.

Effective marketing communications professionals take note of these differences and craft their contributions to communicate directly with each group involved in the buying decision. For example, when presenting to senior management, you want your marketing communications to emphasize those factors that are important to management, which are typically not the same factors that are important to the engineers or manufacturing people. These messages are consistent at all levels of the organization, but they respond to the specific needs and wants of the differing decision makers. The application matrix can be expanded to include the different groups of people and to show how marketing communications intends to communicate with each group.

Sales Goals by Product Line and Market Segment

The last piece in this part of the marketing puzzle is to articulate the sales goals for each product line for each market segment. These goals contribute to volume and market share goals for each product line and can be added to the application matrix. If you are going to use an elec-

Q4'95 Sales Goals by Product Line by Segment (000s)				
Product Line: LA	**Served Market: Legal**			
Application	**Partner**	**Attorney**	**Paralegal**	**Office Staff**
Initial Capability				
Model a	–	–	–	15
Model b	–	–	–	10
Model c	–	–	–	20
Correspondence				
Model d	–	–	–	10
Model e	–	–	–	10
Model f	–	–	–	10
Client Billing				
Model d	–	–	–	15
Model e	–	–	–	20
Model f	–	–	–	20
Totals				
Model a				15
Model b				10
Model c				20
Model d				25
Model e				30
Model f				30

Exhibit 8.2

Sales Goals by Product Line by Segment

tronic spreadsheet to record information, the matrix might get a little large, so you may want to construct another matrix. Another option is to add the additional elements to the spreadsheet and then use the software's "hide" function to hide the rows and columns until needed. Exhibit 8.2 uses two matrices—one for the office staff segment and one for the six models designed to address the three applications (initial capability, correspondence, and client billing) to illustrate this concept.

If your company has prior experience with the same or related product lines, it is helpful to map the effectiveness of prior positioning efforts to the segment goals. This requires showing the relationship between previous marketing communications efforts and the resulting sales volume. While it is often difficult to conclude that specific ads caused an increase in sales, we can look at the patterns in the data. One technique that works quite well is a type of analysis called the Average Experience Model (AEM).

Suppose, for example, that you want to get an idea of the pattern of increased sales that might be expected following the initiation of a major advertising campaign. Your sales volume goals by segment call for a substantial increase in sales and you want to know how effective advertising has been in the past. The first thing to do is to gather the sales data for a period of time preceding and following the initiation of the ad campaign. The sales for the period before the campaign is the baseline, and the sales for the period following the campaign is related to the campaign's effectiveness. The data are first seasonally adjusted to compensate for any chance occurrences of increased volume due to introduction date. Next, the data are indexed to a common date and given a value of 100. If multiple ad campaigns have been run for related product lines, the average increase in sales for each month following the introduction date is the best estimate of a new campaign's effectiveness.

Chapter 9

Target Account Identification

Once the market segments have been defined and the application matrix constructed, the next step is to identify the prospective target accounts. The criteria for target account identification are generally different for each market served, but the process is the same across all segments. For example, a fundamental criterion is that the prospective accounts must collectively have the potential to satisfy your company's sales goals. For example, if the strategic marketing plan calls for revenue to grow at a 15 percent annual rate, you probably want high-growth companies in the list of prospective target accounts. If your served markets are populated with fast-growth companies, perhaps some additional criteria for consideration would be:

- In the top ten of their market
- Technology or business leaders
- Revenue greater than $100 million
- Historic revenue growth greater than 15 percent per year
- Historic earnings growth greater than 5 percent per year
- Early adopters of specific technologies
- Centers of influence or enablers to other served markets

Of course, many additional criteria can be applied depending on the goals and objectives of your company. Defining the criteria that are to be met by the prospective target accounts is a critical first step in developing a target account approach to your served markets. To conduct this first-level analysis, marketing tacticians must have ready access to extensive databases, preferably in electronic form. There are many sources for this information.

Sources of Information

Like the market data in the previous chapter, much information on prospective accounts is available in the reference section of your local public or university library. Sometimes libraries offer it in electronic form, but often they only carry it in print media—large books. Still, if your company is small or your budget limited, the information can be obtained, but it will take a little more work and a lot more time than using an electronic database.

Nonelectronic Sources

Examples of nonelectronic sources of information on prospective accounts include the following:

- *America's Corporate Families* (corporate linkage and ownership)
- *Dun's Business Rankings*
- *Dun's Directory of Service Companies*
- *Electronics Manufacturers Directory*
- *High-Technology Market Place Directory*
- *Hoover's Master List of U.S. Companies*
- *Million Dollar Directory: American's Leading Public and Private Companies*
- *Moody's Industrial Manual*
- *National Directory of Women-Owned Business Firms*
- *Standard & Poor's Register of Corporations, Directors and Executives*

Most, if not all, of these sources will contain information about the firm's name, size, location, and types of products or services offered. Some will have names of key executives. The names, however, are usually out-of-date.

Electronic Sources

If you have a larger budget, you can probably afford to purchase extensive databases on CD-ROM or purchase floppy disks containing specialized listings. Often, the companies that publish the databases also offer custom search services. If your target account criteria are well defined, it may well be worthwhile to commission a custom search and have the company ship you the data in a format that is compatible with your software.

As examples, we offer descriptions of three different commercial sources: *Business Marketplace, CorpTech*, and *Selectory*.

Business Marketplace is a CD-ROM product that contains the broadest source of businesses with approximately nine million records. Each record represents a company and includes such specifics as company name, location, type of ownership, phone, year started, annual sales, number of employees, type of business (SIC codes), and name and title of principal officer. The CD-ROM is common to both Windows and Macintosh systems. Operating software provided with the product allows you to build lists of companies using criteria you have developed.

CorpTech supplies a directory of high-technology companies in the United States in both print and electronic media. Their database contains over 40,000 companies and includes information on parent companies. CorpTech will also conduct custom searches using your criteria. The content is similar to that of Business Marketplace although the company and product descriptions are more detailed plus they have a proprietary coding system that extends the basic SIC codes. CorpTech also offers regional databases.

Selectory is a database of U.S. and international electronics manufacturers with ten or more employees and is the combined efforts of Harris Publishing and Scott's Directories. The disks come packaged with Knowledge Access International's retrieval system. Content is similar to Business Marketplace and CorpTech with a few additions. Selectory provides three categories of import/export data: firms that import products from other countries, firms that export products to other countries, and firms that do both. Selectory also lists defense contractors in the United States. The search software can perform Boolean Logic searches involving AND/OR plus WILD CARD searches.

Purchase of all three sources presented in this section would cost about $2000. This modest cost is returned a hundred-fold when you consider the dollar value of the time saved by your salespeople when they are no longer asked to prospect. The added advantage of using electronic sources of information is that the data that meet your criteria can be mapped to your company's various sales territories. This can help you to evaluate the sales coverage by defined territory.

Identifying Target Accounts

The three sources presented above all provide the capability for searching the databases using your search criteria. Your goal is to apply the criteria generated in your planning and search the tens of thousands of existing businesses to produce a list of prospective accounts that meet or exceed your criteria. Some databases permit a Boolean search to combine criteria in an AND/OR and sometimes NOR combination. For those databases that do not provide Boolean search, you can execute a search using one or more criteria and build a list of those records that match your criteria. You can then search the resulting list using additional criteria to find the records that meet the combined criteria.

The practicality of producing lists from lists is highlighted when you are asked to produce separate lists of prospective accounts for each of your company's sales territories. Working from a master list made up from all geographic areas, all manner of sublists can be generated with very little effort. We will use the concept of sets to illustrate how a complex list of prospective accounts can be built up over several searches. Most databases contain several searchable fields. The sample fields shown below have been reproduced from *Harris Selectory Electronics Manufacturers Directory on Disc.*

- Area code
- City
- Company name

- Country
- County
- Headquarters' information
- Import/export
- Military
- Number of employees
- Ownership
- Personnel titles
- Plant size
- Product alpha
- Product keyword (wildcard available)
- Postal code (Canada)
- SIC (all)
- SIC (primary only)
- Sales revenue
- State/province
- Year established
- Zip code (U.S.)
- User added field 1
- User added field 2

Many databases allow group searches or single searches that can then be constructed into multiple sets. A group search is a search in which a number of fields are searched concurrently, such as city, Zip code, number of employees, and primary SIC code. Executing a search defined in this manner will return only those records that meet *all* of your criteria. An alternate search strategy is to use a single criterion or multiple criteria to generate lists of records that could then be combined or cross-searched in any number of ways. One example of this type of search addresses the need to produce separate lists of prospective accounts for each of the company's sales territories.

When you apply this type of search strategy, the response to each of your searches is called a *set*. For example, if you search the database and identify all companies whose annual sales revenue is equal to or greater than $50 million, then only those records that meet or exceed your criterion will be identified in the first set. If you are then interested in conducting a second search, say, on primary SIC code equal to 3674 (semiconductors), then a second set will be created. This same process can go on and on depending on the level of detail desired in each set.

The sets can usually be cross-searched in three different ways using the Boolean Operators AND, OR, and NOT. AND combines the records from the lists, OR identifies those records that are in both lists, and NOT identifies those records that are in the first list but not in the second. The NOT operator allows you to search one list against another. For example, the NOT operator can be used to identify those records that are in list 1 and not in list 2—or to identify those records that are in list 2 and are not in list 1. Using these Boolean Operators, many different sublists can be constructed.

Constructing the Target Account Profile

Once the prospective target accounts have been identified, individual target account profiles can be constructed. The contents of the profile depend on the use to which the profile will be put. It is possible to construct a master account profile that is maintained by marketing with abbreviated versions distributed to the field sales force. The master target account profile should contain information as shown in Exhibit 9.1. Looking ahead, the master account profile could also contain information about served markets, strategic relationships, and competition.

Profiling the Competition

The same process is used to construct a profile of the competition. Once the basics are in place, additional information can be added. Information about technologies, product lines, served markets, sales history at each prospective target account, share-of-market at each account, product data sheets, product features and benefits, prices,

Target Account Profile	Created: 6/3/95 Last Revised: 6/3/95

Name and Location:

Doble Engineering Co.   Ownership: Private
85 Walnut Street   Formed: 1983
Watertown, MA 02172   Annual Sales: $50mm
Phone: (617) 555-4900   No. of Employees: 450
Fax: (617) 555-0528

Company Description:

Manufacturer of electrical apparatus testing equipment. The power factor test equipment analyzes the insulation of electrical transformers. The circuit breaker analyzers measure the voltage of electrical boxes. The relay test equipment analyzes electricity over long distances. Products are sold to the electric utility industry.

Product SIC Codes:

3829, Relay Test Equipment
3829, Power Factor Test Equipment
3820, Circuit Breaker Analysis

Key Personnel:

Gloria Hernandez, President and CEO
Joyce Caruthers, VP Marketing
Larry Nordit, VP Finance
Phil Brooks, VP Engineering
Lon Thim, Sales Manager
Renatta Quintero, Export Manager

Our Principal Competition:

1st: Bergdorf Analytics @ 15.0% share
2nd: Adelphi Systems @ 10.0% share

Exhibit 9.1

Target Account Profile

quality and reliability, news releases, and the names and backgrounds of each key employee. Like the master target account profile, portions of the competitor profile can be made available to different people in your organization based on their needs and the situation at hand. For example, in a competitive bid situation or a major contract review, you will want as much information available as possible. Exhibit 9.2 illustrates how a competitor profile might look.

Competitor Profile	Created: 6/3/95	Last Revised: 6/3/95

Name and Location:

Bergdorf Analytics
213 Wilson Avenue
Cheshire, CT 06410
Phone: (213) 555-5431
Fax: (213) 555-0445

Ownership: Public
Formed: 1987
Annual Sales: $500 mm
No. of Employees: 4200

Company Description:

Manufacturer of electronic circuit boards for test equipment manufacturers. Specializes in the integration of high current applications. Circuit boards are rated for highly contaminated environments. Products are field changeable by skilled electric utility employees.

Product SIC Codes: **Key Personnel:**

3672, Printed Circuit Boards

William John, President and CEO
Jolene Edwards, VP Marketing
Art Muldauer, VP Finance
Rebecca Traub, VP Engineering
Tom Arbor, Sales Manager
Mercedes Garcia, Export Manager

Major Product Lines:

Eagle Double-Sided Boards, 60% of revenue
BG High-Density Boards, 40% of revenue

Exhibit 9.2

Competitor Profile

Developing the Sales Kit

The sales kit is not a single physical entity. The contents of the sales kit are electronic and are constructed from a variety of sources depending on the prospective account, emerging sales opportunities, competition, product lines, and the planned engagement strategy. This approach results in the greatest degree of flexibility, lowest cost, and the greatest confidence that the latest and most accurate information is being used.

The target account and competitor profiles are constructed and maintained by marketing tacticians using a master profile to facilitate construction. In the same way, master files are created and maintained for each element in the sales kit. As new information about the various elements becomes available, it can be added to the master file and an up-to-date sales kit made available to the users. The individual elements are accessed via the computer network "groupware" software and sales kits are constructed as needed.

For security, the groupware selected should have both password and access authorization capabilities. Simple version checking on the server computer can check and determine whether the requester has a current version of the elements selected for downloading. If not, the new version can replace the older version. This simple process prevents the use of outdated data sheets, old pricing, and obsolete presentations. The goal is for marketing tacticians to construct these sales kits, as needed, for training and then instruct the salespeople on how the different elements can be accessed depending on the prospective account, competition, level of sales presentation required, and type of engagement strategy adopted. The sales kit is the formal information link between marketing and sales as well as the vehicle used by tactical marketing to train the sales force.

The sales kit contains all the information the salesperson needs when calling on, qualifying, and developing the account. Using standard software found in Microsoft Office or Lotus SmartSuite, marketing tacticians construct multiple slide presentations to support the different types of sales presentations required in a complex sale. Sample spreadsheets are included and photographs embedded as needed. Supporting documentation, customer testimonials, technical white papers, and the like can also be included as required. Printing costs, inventories, and distribution delays are eliminated by the electronic sales kit. In Part V, "Staying on Track", we will discuss target account reviews and business won/business lost analyses. During these reviews the contents of the sales kits are validated or modified based on the sales results.

Chapter 10

Engagement Strategy

The engagement strategy describes the basic approach to be used in calling on, qualifying, and developing the target account. Marketers should take several factors into consideration when establishing the engagement strategy. These factors include the markets served, how they are segmented, potential applications, and the procurement cycle of the target account. Another key factor that is often overlooked is the type of prospective account.

Types of Accounts

Prospective accounts can be grouped into four broad categories: existing accounts and existing products; existing accounts and new products; new accounts and existing products; and new accounts and new products. Each of these four categories requires a different engagement strategy.

Existing Accounts and Existing Products

With existing accounts and existing products, you have the greatest history in your relationship both as a company and in terms of the products and services supplied. The history is influenced by your company's prior performance in the four broad areas of price, quality, performance, and delivery and may be positive, neutral, or negative. In reality, there are multiple histories, and each of these many histories must be taken into consideration when developing an effective engagement strategy for these accounts. For example, at one level is the question of whether the many customers within the account view your company as a trusted, reliable, and responsible supplier. At another level, the history is influenced by the customers' perceptions of your products. Did they perform as stated and advertised? Were they priced equitably? Did they meet the customers' expectations of quality? In terms of histories and relationships, this category is the most complex.

Existing Accounts and New Products

In the category of existing accounts and new products, products were supplied previously. All of the concerns raised in the first category apply here as well. The account history must be taken into consideration when crafting the engagement strategy for these accounts. In those cases in which some of the histories are negative, for example, you must do some remedial work. For example, consider an account for which the delivery history includes a problem involving some of the previous products. In this case the engagement strategy should include a dialogue or presentation that initiates discussion about previous delivery performance, how that has affected our relationships, and what we are doing about the problem. Positive histories, too, are to be taken into consideration and utilized in the engagement strategy.

New Accounts and Existing Products

With new accounts for which the sales opportunities involve existing products, there are no direct histories and no relationships. In this case, the engagement strategy must introduce yourself, your role, your company, and your products. With new accounts, the prospective customers want to know about the strength, reliability, and integrity of your company. Once they believe that your company is trustworthy, they are prepared to hear about your company's products. With existing products, the engagement strategy must provide information about your company as a reliable supplier of high-quality products and services at a fair price. Third-party testimonials are especially appropriate in early engagements with prospective accounts in this category.

New Accounts and New Products

For prospective accounts in the category of new accounts and new products, there is no direct history with your company or with your products. There may, however, be positive or negative perceptions or expectations. In any case, the engagement strategy includes the opportunity for some early dialogue about these perceptions. For example, before offering information that your company is a reliable supplier, first ask what the customers within the target account know about your company and your products. Listen carefully and probe for meaningful details and greater understanding. Gear your presentation to the perceptions shared and then schedule a follow-up meeting to present other capabilities.

The Buying Decision Matrix

The buying decision matrix, shown in Exhibit 10.1, is a four-fold table that serves as a useful summary of the characteristics of buying decisions with different levels of complexity. Products requiring a complex sale involve complex buying decisions. The decisions are somewhat different based on the type of account.

For *existing accounts and existing products* and where the company and product histories are positive, the buying decision is often routine and may involve only a few people. Because of the positive histories, the buying decision is perceived as a low risk event that generally requires little or no additional supporting information from the supplier. The larger accounts may rely on an approved vendor list (AVL) with standard pricing. Servicing these types of accounts requires your company to provide timely and accurate information on product availability and on-time deliveries of quality products. The decision maker is almost always the end user. Purchasing agents will only get involved when a new contract period rolls around or when they wish to reopen discussions about price or other terms.

Products

Existing   New

Accounts

Existing

Routine Decision

- Routine decision if history positive
- Perceived low risk decision
- Requires little additional information
- Rely on approved vendor list (AVL)
- May negotiate price concessions
- Decision maker usually end user

Little Complexity

- Involves small groups of people
- Perceived moderate risk decision
- Some additional technical information requested (white papers)
- Decision makers usually include purchasing, manufacturing and engineering

New

Some Complexity

- Multiple small groups involved
- Company information important
- Company reputation a factor
- Perceived moderate risk decision
- Competitive comparisons key
- Senior management involved
- Decision makers usually include purchasing and manufacturing

Much Complexity

- Many different groups involved
- Relatively long selling cycle
- Perceived high risk decision
- Requires much information
- Competitive comparisons
- Samples and testing required
- Decision makers usually include engineering and management

Exhibit 10.1

The Buying Decision Matrix

Existing accounts and new products, where the company and product histories are positive, are similar to the first category but usually involve additional people. The risk is perceived as moderate and therefore the same group of people will often request additional information to support their decision. They may be interested in white papers describing the performance parameters of the new products. The people involved in the buying decision in these types of accounts are usually manufacturing and purchasing agents. For technical products, engineering is often involved.

New accounts and existing products also involve small groups of people in the buying decision. It is important to understand the new accounts' perceptions of your company and product histories. If they are neutral or negative, the perceptions must be addressed before any decisions will be made. The customers will also be interested in comparisons between your company's products and those of your competition. Senior management may be involved in the early stages, but usually the buying decisions are delegated to people in purchasing and manufacturing.

The last category, *new accounts and new products,* involves a great deal of time and multiple meetings and presentations to multiple groups of people. The decision-making process is complex, and the complexity is amplified by variance in knowledge and understanding by the people involved. A consistent message across the various organizational levels is critical for understanding and support. Usually a large amount of information is required, and you can expect the prospective new account to be shopping the competition. For these types of accounts, engineering and management are the key decision makers.

The Engagement Strategy Matrix

The engagement strategy matrix, shown in Exhibit 10.2, establishes the general approach for engaging each type of account. For example, for a new account and new product opportunities, the initial engagement strategy calls for the arrangement of a meeting with the senior manage-

	Existing Account Histories			New Account Info			White Paper	Letters	Competitive Benchmark
	Sales	Service	Applications	Finance	Technical	Map			
Existing Account Existing Product	X	X	X	N/A	N/A	N/A	X	X	X
Existing Account New Product			X	N/A	X	X	X	X	X
New Account Existing Product	N/A	N/A	X	X	X	X	X	X	X
New Account New Product	N/A	N/A	X	X	X	X	X	X	X

Exhibit 10.2

Engagement Strategy Matrix

ment of the prospective account to establish the financial credibility and technical capabilities of your company. If your company is a public company, this might involve quarterly and annual reports, SEC filings, analysts' reports, and major financial press clippings. For technical capabilities, it might include a historical technology timeline together with your company's vision for the future. For the initial meeting, don't get too detailed with the technical materials, but present the technology in terms of the perceived needs and wants of the prospective account.

Engagement Strategy and the Sales Kit

When the sales kit is electronic, specific sales kits can be assembled quickly to meet the needs of specific groups of people within each of the categories of prospective accounts. Constructing a relationship between the engagement strategy, the type of account, and the product lines helps the salesperson to select the presentation that satisfies the identified engagement strategy and to select the appropriate selling cycle and structured approach to qualifying and developing the account.

Defining the Selling Cycle

The selling cycle is a structured approach to calling on, qualifying, developing, and closing the many sales opportunities at each of the prospective target accounts. The selling cycle differs somewhat based on the type of account, the opportunity defined, and the product line selected. For products and services requiring a complex sale, the length of the selling cycle can range from as short as a few weeks to as long as a few years. The median selling cycle is probably somewhere between three to nine months. Many inexperienced salespeople will try to move the sale along too quickly and will thereby jeopardize the success of the sale. Expert salespeople know there is a preferred sequence and a preferred time between the steps in the selling cycle for the major cat-

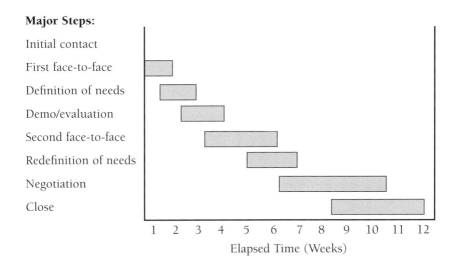

Major Steps:

Initial contact

First face-to-face

Definition of needs

Demo/evaluation

Second face-to-face

Redefinition of needs

Negotiation

Close

Elapsed Time (Weeks)

Exhibit 10.3

Sample Selling Cycle

egories of products. The task is to discover that preferred cycle for your company's products.

If you do not yet have accurate product line records for your company's top salespeople, you can convene a panel of expert salespeople to ask their opinion on the critical steps in the selling cycle for the company's major product lines. At the same time, ask them about the minimum and maximum time desired between the steps. A sample form is useful for these discussions. Exhibit 10.3 contains such a sample for business-to-business sales of a desktop microcomputer to a target account, which is a new account interested in an existing product.

Communicating with the Sales Organization

In summary, within the context of the relational model and the account development cycle, tactical marketing carries the primary responsibility for market development, account identification, and engagement strategy. Tactical marketing uses the information generated by these three areas of responsibility to communicate with the sales force. The account development cycle provides the necessary focus and the rationale for the communications. When the salespeople see the extent of the thinking that has gone into the development of the market, the identification of prospective accounts, and how best to engage each, they become highly motivated to pursue the account.

Part IV

Sales

Chapter 11

The Role, Responsibilities, and Relationships of Sales

We have described marketing's role in business analysis and planning. Sales builds on the work of marketing and calls on, qualifies, penetrates, and services the target accounts, both existing and new.

The Role of Sales

The salesperson is the primary contact with the customer. Rarely, if ever, should there be any contact with the customer that does not include the salesperson responsible for the account. The salesperson "owns" the account and is focused on the here-and-now. Based on the type of account and the engagement strategy adopted, the salesperson utilizes the sales kit and his or her knowledge and experience to qualify, develop, and service the target accounts. The primary role of sales is to sell *existing* products and services at a level of price, quality, and performance acceptable to customers.

Major Responsibilities

The initial responsibility of sales is to understand the strategies and tactics crafted by marketing for each of the prospective target accounts. This understanding makes the salesperson most effective and is fundamental to the relational model and the account development cycle. For example, when sales is dependent on marketing's identification of prospective target accounts, the salespeople gain about a 15 to 20 percent increase in face-to-face selling time because they are no longer required to prospect.

The salespeople are responsible for using the engagement strategy and sales kit to call on the target accounts and to begin or extend the account development process. The sales kit contains an account profile, data sheets, white papers, testimonials, and sales history if applicable. The salesperson knows who the key players are, knows about the potential sales opportunities, and knows about possible competition before ever calling on the account.

With an account profile in place, account qualification shifts quickly to identifying or verifying the identity of the key decision makers in each of the potential sales opportunities. The salesperson is responsible for clarifying the needs and wants of specific customers and matching those needs and wants to the features and benefits of the most appropriate products. He or she is also responsible for tracking each of the developing sales opportunities through its respective selling cycle. This becomes very important when the time comes to generate bookings or order forecasts. The salesperson is also responsible for improving or refining the selling cycle. For example, the salesperson may find through experience that additional steps in the selling cycle, such as an additional review by another group within the account, would result in increased success.

The sales organization is responsible for chairing and presenting a detailed review of all target accounts on at least a quarterly basis. This includes a brief statement of the business conditions at the account, your position as a supplier, some insight on the competition, and a detailed review of each of the sales opportunities. During the account reviews the salespeople articulate their approach to developing, penetrating, and servicing the account.

Last, but not least, is the responsibility the sales organization has as a resource manager for tactical and strategic marketing. You should *never* ask salespeople to sell products before they are developed and released for sale. The salesperson's role is to sell existing product at a price that is acceptable to the customer. For future products, the salesperson is to function as a resource manager and to arrange the necessary meetings for marketing tacticians (and marketing strategists if needed) with the customers to discuss the company's plans for the future. In addition to scheduling the meeting, the salesperson knows who is to attend and what sorts of questions they will have. The salesperson opens the meeting and reviews its purpose before turning the meeting over to the marketing people. The salesperson also closes the meeting and takes responsibility for any follow-up.

The salesperson should not be responsible for presenting future product plans because he or she has no control over when or if a planned product is to be introduced. When salespeople present future products, the customer holds them responsible if those products are late to market. When the salesperson functions, instead, as a resource manager and allows the marketing people to present the new product plans, his or her credibility is not put at risk.

Relationship to Strategic and Tactical Marketing

Sales' relationships with strategic and tactical marketing are many, varied, and complex. For example, as salespeople develop the target accounts, they are intimately involved with marketing tacticians and depend heavily on them for product training, prospective target account identification, product availability, product positioning, sales kits, and engagement strategies. Salespeople build and maintain their relationships with marketing tacticians through dialogue. For example, salespeople communicate, via the target account reviews, their progress in developing the accounts and how well the engagement strategies and sales kits are working. Their relationships are highly complementary.

Marketing strategists should be present during the target account reviews to learn first-hand about the customers' current and projected needs and wants and how the company's product lines are or are not satisfying them. In these meetings, sales and marketing representatives may collectively decide that marketing strategists should visit a number of customers to learn more about them.

Planning Level and Horizon

The planning horizon for sales consists of multiple time periods. The fiscal year is usually the longest time period and relates more to annual quotas and commissions than to specific target account planning. Some companies pay sales commissions on a yearly as well as a quarterly basis. Within the account development model, it is appropriate to use the fiscal year as a longer-term planning horizon for developing and penetrating specific target accounts. By doing so, the salesperson can keep track of planned sales levels for each major target account.

The next planning horizon is quarterly. Typically, the salesperson is asked to make a commitment to achieving a specific sales revenue for each of the fiscal quarters. With the product selling cycles being about a quarter in length, the better salespeople plan when they want their sales to close and work backward to identify the specific starting point for each opportunity.

Monthly planning is just a refinement of the quarterly planning horizon. Months are important but not as important as quarters. Once again, the more effective salespeople break down their quarterly goals into monthly goals and seek to track their own performance across the months.

Daily and weekly planning horizons are used in conjunction with the longer-term planning. Most of this planning involves making appointments and meeting face-to-face with current and prospective customers.

Forecast Level and Horizon

Many companies require their sales force to generate a detailed forecast each month in units and dollars by customer, by product, by month, and spanning a horizon of six months to three years. Using the relational model and the account development cycle, this is no longer required.

First, executives ask the marketing strategists and tacticians to generate a monthly forecast of potential sales or billings. This removes the need for salespeople to generate a similar forecast. Instead, the salespeople forecast when they are planning to book the orders that they are tracking through their respective selling cycles. This bookings forecast is updated monthly. Operations and manufacturing planning managers then generate a response that takes into consideration the backlog and important inventory information to produce a revenue forecast. In the chapter on target account development, we will expand this concept considerably, once again seeking to take advantage of the relational nature of marketing and sales.

Impact of Information

The information generated by sales organization has the greatest impact on the present and the near term. The success of their account development activities tells the organization how well the customers are accepting the company's product lines. The order booking rate confirms or refutes marketing's forecasts and drives week-to week manufacturing schedules, staffing, and procurement.

Chapter 12

Target Account Qualification

Historically, account qualification followed as a natural consequence of prospecting. Salespersons identified prospective accounts in their territories and during their initial meetings sought to qualify the company and the buyers. These early activities involved learning about the company's finances, identifying the decision makers, and determining if funds were earmarked for certain types of purchases. In the relational approach, account qualification takes on a new meaning. For example, much of the earlier work that was required to qualify the account is now provided for the salesperson in the form of account profiles, competitor profiles, and application matrices. This offers the tremendous advantage of allowing the salesperson to focus on building the critical customer relationships.

Target account qualification is a broad-ranging term that describes the initial process of calling on accounts, determining their interest and financial means to purchase the company's products and services, identifying and quantifying opportunities, and updating the information on the most likely competitors. It also includes developing an understanding of the purchasing process employed by the prospective account, such as purchasing calendar, purchase order cycle, capital appropriations committees, signature levels, and so on. This detailed information becomes very important when the salesperson is asked to modify specific selling cycles.

Applying the Engagement Strategy

The Engagement Strategy Matrix in Chapter 10 is a good guide to planning engagement strategies. These early activities focus on information giving and gathering, not selling per se. When calling on a new account, it is important to establish a relationship with both the formal and the informal organization. For example, to a salesperson, the formal organization is the account's procurement or purchasing function. The people responsible for purchasing usually focus on quality, price, and delivery. They are interested in the financial health of your company and whether or not you are a reliable supplier. If you are new to your industry, then you probably should use the third-party testimonials in the sales kit to attest to your company's financial legitimacy. Customers may not request specific references. This is your first test. When you clear this hurdle, the discussion turns to your products and services.

You already have the target account profile and therefore you have information about the account in terms of their business, markets served, products, and ideally, how your company's products and services can benefit them. This knowledge can help you understand the other aspects of your target's business. Begin to develop an understanding of how your company's products and services can fit in with their goals and objectives.

Understanding the Customer's Business

The most valuable supplier is one who understands the customer's business and takes the initiative in bringing possible solutions to a customer's attention. To do this effectively, you must first understand your customer's business. For example, the application matrix for microcomputers in Chapter 8 (Exhibit 8.1) illustrates different applications for various segments of a law firm.

If you are qualifying a new law firm account, you want to know what type of law they practice. Do they specialize in tax law, estate planning, criminal law, corporate law, personal injury, or labor law? Knowing the type of law practiced tells you the types of problems the account is interested in solving. Add to this the differing needs of the partners, attorneys, paralegals, and staff, and a number of possible applications can be addressed. A similar process can be used when calling on and qualifying any type of target account.

The same concepts apply if you are a designer or manufacturer of active sportswear. To be effective in selling your company's products to your customers, you must know something about your customers. For example, if your targeted market is upscale resorts in the Southwest, you will want to know as much as possible about the people who frequent such resorts. Where do they live? How do they select one resort over another? What are the major activities in which they engage? Are they avid golfers or tennis players? With whom do they socialize? How do they travel? This list of questions could continue for a long time, but the point is to learn as much about your customers' customers as possible. This will only enhance your value to *your* customers.

Identifying Opportunities

From the target account profile, competitor profiles, engagement strategy, application matrix, sales kits, and early dialogue with the customer, you have a great deal of information about the target account. The next step is to frame this information in terms of needs and wants and then to look for a relationship between the customer's needs and wants and the features and benefits of your company's product lines.

Do not "reinvent the wheel." For example, if your marketers have constructed an application matrix, seek first to validate that matrix rather than setting out to develop another. If the marketplace has changed or if there are new product developments, adjust the matrix as appropriate.

Identifying Most Likely Competitors

At this juncture, information about the most likely competitors comes to light. In some cases the customer will tell you who is the major competitor. If the marketing tacticians have done a thorough job in generating the competitor profiles, chances are that you already have information on the most likely competitors. You may need, however, to update the competitor profiles with new information. Knowledge about the competition can give you insights into the account that you do not have. For example, how was the competing company chosen, what relationships do they have in place, how have they been measured, how has their performance been, and so on. The questions are broad and general at this point, but, as we will see in the next chapter, this information gets more and more specific as the account development process unfolds.

Chapter 13

Target Account Development

When the salesperson is qualifying target accounts, he or she is primarily interested in learning about the needs and wants of the account and in exploring ways in which the company's products and services might satisfy them. Target account development, on the other hand, involves the process of identifying and tracking each specific sales opportunity. It includes building the necessary relationships with each of the many customers within the account, identifying specific sales opportunities, linking each opportunity with the appropriate product line, and tracking each opportunity through its respective selling cycle.

Building Relationships

The first order of business in account development is building the necessary relationships with each of the many customers within the account. Perhaps a brief explanation of what we mean by *account* and *customer* is in order. We will use the same law firm example that we used in the application matrix. In this example, the law firm is the account and the partners, attorneys, paralegals, and staff are the different categories of customers. Within each category, specific people become specific customers. Building effective relationships in this context means meeting with and understanding the needs and wants of the specific people within each of the categories.

One good example of an opportunity to build a customer relationship is when the salesperson discovers that different individuals within an account have conflicting needs and wants. This kind of situation gives the salesperson the opportunity to build or strengthen his or her relationship with both the group and the individual members. It gives the salesperson a chance to demonstrate a concern for the needs and wants of the individuals and for the group as a whole by helping them work through their differences. The result can be an effective relationship built on interest, trust, and competence. Building the multiple relationship required to be successful in a complex sales environment can take considerable time and effort. The engagement strategy matrix provides an effective guide to the process. For example, new accounts and new products usually require the longest time because there are no prior relationships that can be built upon.

Effective relationships permit the resolution of issues before they reach crisis proportions and are most important when there is disagreement, conflict, or "bad news." It is important to realize that effective relationships do not necessarily result in agreements, nor do they mean that the customer is always right. Sometimes the customer is wrong and the salesperson must figure out a way to work through the issue.

Identifying Specific Sales Opportunities

Identifying specific sales opportunities is a genuine art. It requires listening to the customers' stated needs and wants, an understanding of the account's business, and comparing those needs and wants with the features and benefits of your company's products. We will use microcomputers and the law firm example once again to demonstrate.

The application matrix in Exhibit 8.1 indicates six types of models that could be used by staff, paralegals, practicing attorneys, and partners. For office staff and paralegals, models g,h, and i are recommended; for the practicing attorneys, models m,n, and o; for the partners, models j, k, and l. Within any given segment—for example, practicing attorneys—the difference between the models recommended is basically CPU speed, amount of RAM, size of hard drive, and telecom security features. Practicing attorneys often take their computers with them to clients' sites. They usually prefer to load all of their files on the computer so the required capacity of the hard drive is greater than that required by someone who travels less. Another valuable feature is greater random access memory (RAM), which permits the practicing attorney to work within several active files without having to close one or more files or experience slower operation.

By asking questions, listening, and understanding how the law firm functions, the salesperson is able to identify the specific sales opportunity. The opportunity includes supplying 24 Model 1 notebook systems to the partners and 60 Model n notebook systems to the practicing attorneys. Both models selected contain "Kwik-Konfigure" telecom capability that enables the attorneys to synchronize and exchange files wirelessly between their desktop and notebook computers. This simple feature allows them to have, for example, the latest drafts of their important contracts, a summary of their monthly billings to date, and their unanswered e-mail messages at hand.

Selecting Product Lines

Application matrices are helpful but, in the final analysis, the product line is selected from an understanding of the needs and wants of the customers within the account. In the example above, the salesperson selected the LA product line as the product line most suited to meet the needs and wants of the law firm. Why the LA product line? First, the salesperson knew from previous meetings with the different customers (partners and practicing attorneys) that the attorneys traveled a lot, usually had multiple pieces of luggage, and usually checked in for messages while waiting in private airline clubs. These needs indicated product features such as small size, lightweight, ease of use (special features launched with quick keys), and passive file synchronization (all computers equipped with proprietary remote-control file-transfer software).

Some sales organizations are attempting to automate the product selection process by providing their salespeople with product catalogs on CD-ROM. The salesperson can search the product catalog using specific features or key words searches. Once again, specific product line information is contained in sales support tools such as the application matrix, white papers, satisfied customer testimonials, and other valuable aids in the sales kit. Maintaining and using information from previously successful sales efforts develops into a competitive advantage.

The Selling Cycle

The selling cycle is the key to successful target account development. Each product line and served market has its own preferred cycle or sequence of activities that, when followed, tends to yield favorable sales results. The selling cycle is further complicated by the type of target account being developed. New accounts, for example, require extra steps and additional time regardless of the product lines involved. These extra steps permit the salespeople to introduce themselves and offer the prospective customers information about your company.

Broadly speaking, the sequence of the selling cycle begins with a general introduction of people, companies, and products. In these early steps, questions are asked about philosophy, performance, quality, reliability, and price. These conversations tend to be rather general. The opportunity for more specific discussions arises only when the participants feel that there is a potential fit between the people, products, and companies. For some companies, these early meetings take a considerable amount of time and effort, usually consisting of one- to- two-hour meetings with people throughout the organization. Having slides or overheads in the sales kit that are geared to the differing needs and wants of the various groups is valuable and saves a considerable amount of the salesperson's time.

During these early meetings, the more effective salespeople ask a lot of questions and seek to learn who the customers are, what their needs and wants are, the names and titles of the person or persons who can make the decision, and how the prospective company goes about its decision making process. Exhibit 13.1 shows an example of a general selling cycle used by a major account rep for a microcomputer manufacturer. The steps listed are checkpoints. Additional steps too detailed to track and too specific to list occur within these steps. For example, ID/Confirm Decision Maker may include several meetings with people at different levels of the organization. This sequence helps the account rep effectively track his progress.

The length of the individual horizontal bars relates to the average length of time a given step takes to accomplish. Knowing the time required to accomplish specific tasks enables the salesperson to

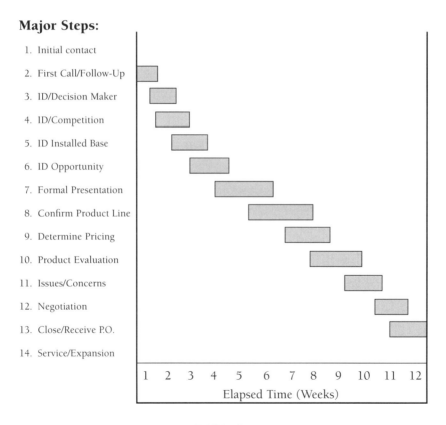

Major Steps:

1. Initial contact
2. First Call/Follow-Up
3. ID/Decision Maker
4. ID/Competition
5. ID Installed Base
6. ID Opportunity
7. Formal Presentation
8. Confirm Product Line
9. Determine Pricing
10. Product Evaluation
11. Issues/Concerns
12. Negotiation
13. Close/Receive P.O.
14. Service/Expansion

Elapsed Time (Weeks)

Exhibit 13.1

A Selling Cycle

schedule his or her personal selling time more effectively. Knowing the overall time it takes for the salesperson to progress through the selling cycle also gives sales management insight into whether they will achieve their sales quota. The selling cycle can also be used to review sales effectiveness and improve the accuracy of bookings forecasts.

Using the Sales Kit

The electronic sales kit described previously contains all the information the salesperson needs when calling on, qualifying, and developing the account, including multiple slide presentations, sample spreadsheets, and photographs. For example, when presenting to senior management, the salesperson may emphasize financial data, but he or she will focus on technical information when selling to engineers. However, the messages are consistent at all levels of the organization.

Anticipating Competitors' Responses

Many companies learn about their competition only after they have been told that they didn't get a sale. Even though you cannot control your competition, you should know the strengths and weaknesses of your competitors, their products, and their marketing and salespeople. It is only through this knowledge that you can anticipate their responses to your account development activities. This information should be included in the sales kit and made available to salespeople during training and later for their use in the field.

It is also helpful to know and understand your competitors' selling cycles. Are they about the same as yours? Are their salespeople as effective? Knowledge of their marketing and sales process plus training on expected competitive responses provides an opportunity for your salespeople to further differentiate your company's products from those of your competition. They should not mention the competitor or criticize their products. They should simply use the knowledge to amplify the competitive advantages of your company and your company's products, focusing on the strengths and assets your company brings to the target account.

Forecasting Orders

We have come to an important topic: sales forecasting. As mentioned previously, salespeople should not be asked to forecast unconstrained demand for each of the customers within their territory. To do so is a waste of their time. Not only are they ill-equipped for such a task, the customers often do not know what their future demand will be. For the salesperson to spend the time needed to generate such a forecast reduces their valuable face-to-face selling time. So how does one get a sense of the flow of future orders?

Most manufacturing firms maintain a backlog of unfilled orders. (Note: this is not a stock-out situation.) Products include the full spectrum of manufactured goods from toys to garments to chemicals to furniture and many others. Customers typically place orders with specific quantities subject to release for shipment at a later date or dates. The size of the backlog is reported in units and dollars, as well as equivalent weeks or months of backlog at current shipping rates. Either way, backlog accuracy and good backlog management are very important to the future of the business. Backlogs increase when incoming orders outpace shipments and decrease when shipments exceed orders. Perhaps the best-known backlog measure is the Booked-to-Billed Ratio reported by the semiconductor industry. A ratio of, 1.2 (1:1.2) for example, indicates that for every dollar shipped, 1.2 dollars were booked. This is an increasing backlog. A ratio less than one indicates a shrinking backlog.

Demand for high-tech products usually contains monthly random variance of 10 to 20 percent or more. With monthly production unit volume in the millions, a built-in forecast-versus-actual error of 10 to 20 percent is significant and represents a substantial problem for the operating managers. To reduce this error and improve the precision of the forecast, we take a multi-stage approach to forecasting. Recall from our discussions about strategic and tactical marketing that those functions are responsible for product-line-level revenue forecasts. The salespeople are responsible for identifying and tracking emerging sales opportunities at the target accounts, information about specific product models, configurations, unit volume, prices, and delivery dates. The goal is to blend these two different sets of data to generate a timely and accurate forecast. First, we will look at the selling cycle.

Using the example from Exhibit 13.1 and counting the initial contact as step 1, there are 13 steps in the selling cycle. The list below shows numbers that reflect the cumulative probability of a successful close at each step in the cycle.

Step	Cumulative Probability of Close
1. Initial contact	0.1
2. First call/follow-up	0.2
3. ID/confirm decision makers	0.3
4. ID/confirm	0.3
5. ID installed base	0.4
6. ID opportunity/needs	0.5
7. Formal presentation	0.6
8. Confirm product line	0.7
9. Determine pricing	0.7
10. Demo/product evaluation	0.8
11. Issues/concerns	0.8
12. Negotiation	0.9
13. Close/receive P.O.	1.0

We also know, on average, how long it takes to move from any step in the selling cycle to the close. Knowing this allows you to select the forecast horizon. Remember that these forecasts are bookings or orders that will enter the backlog, so longer term *demand* forecasts from the salespeople are no longer needed. Operations benefit because near term production schedules can be generated from the backlog using a known mix and volume of products.

Chapter 14

Target Account Service and Expansion

Products and services that require a complex sale also require complex service. The seeds of expansion are sown in after-sales service. If service is shoddy, future sales will be seriously jeopardized. If service consistently meets and exceeds the needs and wants of the customers, additional sales opportunities will emerge. The varied customers within the accounts require personalized attention to their specific needs and wants if they are to be satisfied. Three main categories are usually involved in service: price, delivery, and quality.

Performance to Plan

Performance to Plan is a broad term that refers to how well and how punctually you and your company have done what you said you would do. It may consist of vague concepts and expectations, or it may be specific, depending on how well discussions were documented during and following the many steps of the selling cycle. It is important to point out that what the salesperson acknowledges to the customer is "do-able" often gets heard by the customer as "will do," and therefore establishes expectations of future service. Effective salespeople summarize their notes following each meeting and highlight those topics to be addressed in after-sale service.

Tracking Deliveries (CRD, OSD, CSD, and ADD)

Today's fast-paced business environment places incredible demands on companies and their ability to deliver their goods and services in a timely manner. This demand expectation increases as customers reduce the number of vendors from whom they buy. Four dates, CRD (customer request date), OSD (original schedule date), CSD (current schedule date), and ADD (actual delivery date) are important measures of delivery effectiveness.

The first two dates, CRD and OSD, not only tell you how well you are satisfying the customers' requested delivery dates but also provide indirect information about future competition. For example, an increase in the difference between the two dates will eventually lower barriers to competition because the delivery needs of the customers are not being met. On the other hand, being able to point out that your company has satisfied the CRD 100 percent of the time will be helpful in the future. Any effective service plan must include some provision for tracking the degree of correspondence between the CRDs and the OSDs.

The second set of dates, current schedule date (CSD) and actual deliver date (ADD), are also important in after-sale service and expansion. Comparing these dates helps evaluate the effectiveness of the factory and the factory scheduling system. These dates are often used as a performance-to-schedule measure by the factories. An important measure to add is the number of times a particular item has been rescheduled and the difference between the OSD and the CSD. Delivery performance is becoming more and more important. It is also important to recognize that the customer concept of on-time delivery does not mean when your company shipped the product, but when the product actually arrives on the customer's dock.

Quality and Reliability

Discussions of quality and reliability can, and have, filled hundreds of books. The purpose here is not to revisit those issues but to call attention to the need for the salesperson to understand the customer's expectations of quality and reliability. In after-sale service and expansion, the task of the salesperson is to translate these expectations into specific goals with measurable results. For microcomputer manufacturers, for example, measures of service quality might include such topics as the following:

- Percentage of computers configured as requested
- Percentage DOA (dead on arrival) or nonfunctional
- Percentage response to service requests within 2 hours
- Percentage of computers down for more that 24 hours

Measures of reliability might include the following topics:

- Percentage of computers with early breakdown
- Percentage of computers that meet or exceed target mean time between failures (MTBF)
- Percentage of computers compatible in factory authorized upgrades

The task of the salesperson is to verify with the customers that these are the key performance items to report on during the quarterly service reviews. Occasionally, some customer companies construct their own rating scales that allow them to compare the performance of one supplier with that of another. Do not take these scales lightly. Future purchase decisions often hang in the balance.

Forecasting Run Rates

Run rates refer to the ongoing ordering and delivery of product over a period of time. Their use is most prevalent in situations where companies supply components to other companies for inclusion in their end products. One example is a microcomputer manufacturer that has won the right to supply a large company with its PC needs over the next year or two. For this company, the decision to purchase a PC is often driven by the hiring of a new employee or the need for some specific function such as word processing or spreadsheets. In these cases, the manufacturer needs the ability to estimate its customer's needs if it is going to be able to meet the customer request date (CRD).

If there is a general contract in place, the terms of the contract usually specify certain minimum monthly or quarterly quantities required for certain price points. In these cases, the contract numbers can often be used to develop the estimated run-rate forecast. If there is no contract but is some ordering history, the best approach is to develop some sort of a trend chart of previous orders and deliveries and present that to the customer for approval and support. If the ordering trend describes a rather shallow upward or downward slope, then some sort of three-month or exponential averaging usually is adequate. The most important point as it relates to account service and expansion is to share these trend charts and run-rate forecasts with the customer in the monthly or quarterly service reviews.

When new accounts are developed, ordering and delivery history usually are not available. In this case, the dialogue generated with the customers regarding product availability is critical. It is highly recommended that the salesperson share company scheduling and manufacturing information with the customers and explain how orders are scheduled, manufactured, and delivered. This initial understanding of the needs of your company's manufacturing function helps the customer understand the process and time required to convert an order into shippable product. It may also be appropriate to agree on an initial order to be placed on the backlog with specific releases required for delivery. The quantity selected is based on the customer's expectations of the quantity of product required to be delivered and within your company's manufacturing cycle. Monthly and quarterly reviews of orders, deliveries, backlogs, and finished goods inventory provides a baseline for continuing as is or modifying the orders.

Resolving Product Issues

Regularly held service reviews provide the opportunity to address issues before they reach crisis proportions. It is helpful if the salesperson sees himself or herself as a resource manager rather than the sole problem-solver. Perhaps the most important elements in issue resolution are relationships and communication. Good relationships are critical to understanding the issues at hand, and effective communication is critical to maintaining forward momentum in the resolution of issues.

The salesperson should discuss service reviews with the customers early in the relationship. It is important to agree on a regular time for these service reviews when all interested parties can be in attendance. The salesperson should discuss the format of the meetings with the customers. It is most effective to adopt the predominant meeting format of the customers, so they are on more familiar ground. In the service review meeting, the goal is to identify what is important from the perspective of the customers, to capture their concerns accurately and succinctly, and to implement solutions to address each of the open issues.

Chapter 15

Technology Confirmation

Technology confirmation is the last step in the account development cycle. It involves reviewing the effectiveness of your company's technology and products from the perspective of the customer. In this process, the salesperson serves as a representative of the customers, and the marketing people are responsible for determining what changes should be made in technology or product. If the relational model is working effectively the salesperson will have a rich cache of information to share with the marketers during this process.

Technology confirmation provides a critical source of information for business growth. Well-organized data from the sales force that focuses on analysis of business won and business lost, identification and description of customer-requested product features, discussion of price versus performance, new product ideas, and future sales opportunities is invaluable in reaffirming or redirecting your company's product planning. Meetings for technology confirmation should not be put off until the end of the year. They should be incorporated into the quarterly account reviews—the more frequent the meetings, the fresher the data regarding what is occurring in the marketplace. The technology confirmation process proceeds from the general to the specific: that is, from served markets to target accounts to applications and finally to specific product issues.

Monitoring Served Markets

The data for technology review should be discussed within the context of the served market, followed by any segmentation. Using the microcomputer examples previously discussed, served markets may be defined as notebook computers, desktop computers, and servers, which might also be segmented by type of business, such as manufacturing, banking, hospitality, and healthcare. The information could be structured and summarized as shown in Exhibit 15.1.

The way in which the information is structured serves to organize subsequent information. For example, if the company wants to pursue server applications in the segments defined, then marketers will consider new product features involving uninterrupted power supply, larger mirrored hard drives, increased security, and built-in file synchrony if the pattern holds true across several different sales territories.

Active participation in these quarterly reviews allows marketing planners to constantly check and reconcile their product development strategies and plans against the developing needs and wants of the various served markets. If a trend appears to be accelerating, marketing

Served Markets			
	Notebook	Desktop	Server
Manufacturing	stronger case dust proof stronger PCMCIA	removable HD's larger HD's built-in NIC	hot back-up large mirrored HD's UPS
Banking	private HD's removable screen	removable HD's more security built-in NIC	more security hot back-up UPS
Hospitality	preconfigured secure HD's network compatible	quick keys built-in NIC	hot back-up removable HD's UPS
Healthcare	clean for surgery file synchrony dockable	file synchrony removable HD's dockable	file synchrony hot back-up UPS

Note: HD stands for hard drives.
    UPS stands for Uninterrupted Power Supply

Exhibit 15.1

Served Market Summary Matrix

planners can ask the salesperson to chair a meeting with key account decision makers to understand their needs and wants in more detail. These meetings also provide the opportunity for strategic alliances and other joint development activities.

Monitoring Target Accounts

During the quarterly meetings, each salesperson reviews his or her respective target accounts. During these reviews, it is very helpful for the salespeople to summarize their top three accounts to confirm or request changes in technology and product features. This serves to verify marketing plans and to keep marketing planners in touch with the needs and wants of the marketplace. Table 15.2 shows a useful format for summarizing target account information. The actions of major competitors should also be discussed. Are the competitors still

Served Market: Manufacturing			
	Notebook Computer	Desktop Computer	Server
Able Inc. (Metals Mfg.)	sealed keyboard dust proof case stronger PCMCIA	sealed HD no floppy drive built-in NIC	hot back-up large mirrored HD's UPS
Baker Corp. (Electronics)	no wireless xfer removable screen locking cables	removable HD's more security audit trail on HD	more security hot back-up built-in NIC
Charlie Co. (Injection Mold)	preconfigured secure HD's rubber corners	quick keys built-in NIC UPS	old file/new file audit removable HD's fault tolerant

Note: HD stands for hard drives.
UPS stands for Uninterrupted Power Supply

Table 15.2
Summary Matrix of Target Account Needs

on the development track that we expected them to be on, or have they shifted priorities and timing?

The salesperson should make no attempt to prioritize the product features requested by the target accounts, but should explain why and how the requested features would be helpful to the customers within the account. This encourages marketing and salespeople to work together to generate new types of solutions for customers' problems.

Application Review

The review of applications addresses questions of product use: How are the customers using our products? What are the different types of applications? Are customers using our products as we intended them to be used, or are they using them in other creative ways? How can we monitor these applications to help confirm our technology and product development direction?

The purpose of applications review is to give marketing planners feedback on the accuracy of their previous analyses and assumptions

Served Market: Manufacturing			
	Notebook	Desktop	Server
Metals Mfg.	job scheduling production reporting job set-up	area reporting area job costs real time costs	auto poll area boxes duplicate databases all drawings stored
Electronics	pre-ship configuration equipment set-up sheets noise free operation	CAD drawings spreadsheets quality database	backlog/forecast job status/reporting change control records
Injection Mold	used on shop floor many users update server files	job routing job status cost accounting	old file/new file audit store all drawings production histories

Exhibit 15.3

Application Summary Matrix

about the products used. This information, coupled with knowledge of how the various target accounts function in their served markets, provides an incredible advantage for offering value-added products and services to customers. Reviewing product applications keeps marketing planners informed about the target account's business. Exhibit 15.3 provides a useful format for reviewing applications across served markets and their respective segments.

Product Issues

Product issues are the lowest level of detail presented in technology confirmation. Product issues refer to customer complaints regarding specific products or product lines. These issues represent immediate opportunities to demonstrate to customers that you and your company are listening and responding to them. Unless there is a problem in the basic design of the product, these issues are usually easy to resolve. Resolving and publicizing that they have been resolved provides a

All Markets/All Segments			
	Notebook (Models l, m, and o)	Desktop (Models a and b)	Server (All Pro/Tect Models)
Configuration	old video drivers junk software RAM missing	old video drivers obsolete software old FAX card	old video drivers obsolete software hard disk not partitioned
Components	carrying case small PCMCIA fragile charger cable loose	obsolete NIC	obsolete NIC
Case/Keyboard	floppy release sticks release latch stiff mold marks in case	slot covers loose	slot covers loose

Exhibit 15.4
Summary Matrix of Product Issues

143

significant opportunity to better serve the needs and wants of the customers and to expand your relationship with them.

Examples falling into this category include loose computer board expansion slot covers, loose connectors, incorrect configuration, obsolete device drivers, and defective components. A summary of product issues provides a cross-section of product quality from the customer's perspective. If these observations do not match with your internal quality data, it is important to find out why. For example, if your company sells through resellers, are they trained in appropriate handling and set-up procedures? Do they have the latest drivers? A structured format for presenting and discussing product issues is provided in Exhibit 15.4. While a few specifics might differ from industry to industry, the process and approach are similar.

Communicating Results

For maximum usability, the information gathered for technology confirmation can be generated and communicated electronically. For example, electronic forms can be designed using Lotus Notes software and separate yet related databases created for subsequent use by marketing strategists, marketing tacticians, and salespeople.

If the salespeople are equipped with notebook computers and the appropriate software, they can develop and present their information using active matrix overhead projection systems. Their files can be linked directly to Notes Databases permitting other interested parties to share the data.

Part V

Staying on Track

Chapter 16

Target Account Reviews

Keeping up with the changing needs and wants of the marketplace is a continuous challenge. One effective way to accomplish this complex task is through the structured account review process. There are many ways to structure and conduct target account reviews. This chapter will outline one approach, provide examples, and discuss how the account review information can be used effectively.

Structuring Account Reviews

Structured target account reviews provide the opportunity to evaluate a given account in depth. They are most effective when held quarterly. This gives adequate time for the salespeople to show significant progress with the defined sales opportunities, and it corresponds with your company's fiscal periods. The account reviews tend to be most effective when held within the first two weeks following the end of the company's fiscal quarter. In this way, detailed data such as backlog, actual shipments, returns, and so on, that are fresh from the fiscal period close can be used in the account review process. Conducting the reviews early in the fiscal quarter also avoids the frantic pace of the quarter-end, and it provides a great opportunity to validate projected sales revenue for the current quarter.

The contents of the account review is as follows:

- Account name and location
- Current business conditions at the account

- Your position at the account
- Sales history
- Account penetration
- Opportunity tracking
- Competitor information
- Ongoing sales strategy

Account Name and Location

Information on account name and location is taken from the target account profile (see Chapter 9, "Target Account Identification") and structured as shown in Exhibit 16.1. By using the existing account profile information, the data are not duplicated. Also, because the account profile is included in the sales kit, the salesperson is always assured of having current information. Another advantage is that information regarding product lines, SIC codes, and key executives can be continuously reviewed.

Business Conditions

Analysis of target account business conditions encompasses the following questions: How well are they (i.e., the target accounts) doing? Are they hiring? Are they expanding as planned? Are they having manufacturing problems? How are their customers viewing them and their products? This section provides a great opportunity to survey overall business conditions by reviewing specific business conditions at each of your company's target accounts. Exhibit 16.2 shows how this portion of the account review might look.

The diffusion index is a measure of percentage change and is computed from the number of companies indicating an increase minus the number indicating a decrease. If the data are captured by individual company, you have the makings of a valuable early warning system.

You may want to consider supplementing the narrative review of business conditions with one of the techniques used by the Federal Reserve to assess current and projected changes in business conditions. Several different surveys are published, but the *Business Outlook Survey*

Target Account Review	Created 6/3/95	Last Revised: 6/3/95

Name and Location:

Doble Engineering Co.   Ownership: Private
85 Walnut Street   Formed: 1983
Watertown, MA 02172   Annual Sales: $50 mm
Phone: (617) 555-4900   No. of Employees: 450
Fax: (617) 555-0528

Company Description:

Manufacturer of electrical apparatus testing equipment. The power factor test equipment analyzes the insulation of electrical transformers. The circuit breaker analyzers measure the voltage of electrical boxes. The relay test equipment analyzes electricity over long distances. Products are sold to the electric utility industry.

Product SIC Codes:

3829, Relay Test Equipment
3829, Power Factor Test Equipment
3820, Circuit Breaker Analysis

Key Personnel:

Gloria Hernandez, President and CEO
Jerry Jodice, VP Marketing
Larry Nordit, VP Finance
Phil Brooks, VP Engineering
Lou Thim, Sales Manager
Renatta Quintero, Export Manager

Our Principal Competition:

1st: Bergdorf Analytics @ 15.0% share
2nd: Adelphi Systems @ 10.0% share

Exhibit 16.1

Target Account Review

published by the Federal Reserve Bank of Philadelphia is particularly useful. When the format is used for a single account, the percentages are replaced with "1's" and "0's". A "1" would be placed in the column indicating the type of change, and a "0" would be in the others. For example, say new orders were decreasing at a single account. To convey that information, a "1" would be placed at the intersection of new orders and decrease. Zeros would appear under "no change" and "increase" and a "−1" would appear in the diffusion index. Exhibit 16.3

Business Conditions & Position   Created 6/3/95   Last Revised: 6/3/95

Current Business Conditions:
Doble Engineering has been growing in excess of 25% per year for the last two years. Their new line of circuit breaker analyzers are being used by builders of upscale homes as they move more and more to computerized load control centers and computerized security systems. As housing starts jump around, we can expect some volatility. Right now, they look strong.

Position at the Account:
We have about 30% of the account, with Bergdorf at 40% and Adelphi at 30%. We were recently given a superior vendor performance award for both Notebook and Desktop Product Lines. They like our quality but have some concerns about our flexibility and responsiveness to special packaging and delivery requests. They see a lot of volatility in their markets and want us to prepackage and ship directly to the builders.

Sales History (in thousands of dollars):

Product Line	1993	1994	1995	1996	1997	1998	1999
				Forecasts			
Notebooks	1220	1550	1900	2400	3100	4100	5300
Desktops	850	925	1000	1200	1500	1750	2000
Total	2070	2475	2900	3600	4600	5850	7300

Account Penetration:

	Notebooks	Desktops	Servers
Total Account Purchases (TAP)	6300	3500	500
Served Account Purchases (SAP)	6300	3000	0
Share of Account Purchases (SOP)	1900	1000	0

Figure 16.2

Current Business Conditions and Your Position at the Account

Business Outlook Survey				June 1995			
General Condition:							
	June vs. May			6 months from now vs. June			
	(−)	N/C	(+)	Diffusion Index	(−)	N/C	(+)	Diffusion Index
What is your evaluation of the level of general business activity?	34.6	55.0	10.3	−24.3	26.6	33.6	31.7	5.0
Business Indicators:								
New Orders	36.5	46.1	15.9	−20.6	21.4	46.3	32.2	10.8
Shipments	29.7	50.2	17.4	−12.3	25.8	43.6	30.0	4.2
Unfilled Orders	35.2	51.6	10.0	−25.2	31.2	47.7	16.8	−14.4
Delivery Time	28.8	63.5	7.6	−21.2	16.0	68.9	13.8	−2.2
Inventories	31.3	42.1	26.3	−5.0	32.1	41.9	24.0	−8.1
Prices Paid	8.5	60.4	31.1	22.5	5.1	56.1	38.9	33.8
Prices Received	13.1	77.2	9.7	−3.5	9.3	55.2	35.3	26.1
No. of Employees	20.9	74.6	4.4	−16.5	27.7	58.1	14.3	−13.4
Avg. Work Week	25.0	66.3	6.1	−18.9	18.0	60.9	19.3	1.2
Capital Expenditures	−	−	−	−	23.7	41.2	13.0	−10.7

Exhibit 16.3

Business Outlook Survey

shows, for example, the numbers reported in the June 1995 issue of the Philadelphia Fed's *Business Outlook Survey.*

Your Position at the Account

Your position at the account encompasses the following questions: Is your company seen as a valued and trusted supplier or do you have a history of late deliveries? How do customers at the account view your product quality and price? Do you have a strong history of good service?

Sales History

In the sales history review, you summarize your company's sales history to the account by major product lines. This shows the significance of this particular account to your company's overall business. We recommend two years of history and projections for the current year, and four additional years. The current year's numbers are what the salespeople are working toward, and the five-year window is based on the strategic and tactical marketing forecasts. Units and/or dollars can be used. Although we have shown dollars, it is usually better to use units so the numbers do not have to be continually adjusted for inflation.

Account Penetration

A discussion of account penetration analysis requires some definitions. Chapter 6 used the terms *TAM* (total available market), *SAM* (served available market), and *SOM* (share of market) in discussions of markets and how they are segmented. The discussion of individual accounts will use a similar yet slightly different set of terms. The purpose of a review of account penetration is to find out the total amount of a particular product line being purchased by the account and, of that total, what share the company has. New terms are used here to prevent confusion with the marketing terms: *TAP* (total account purchases), *SAP* (served account purchases), and *SOP* (share of account purchases). The SAP line refers to that subset of the total purchases that are manufactured by your company. SOP is computed as a percentage of SAP.

Opportunity Tracking

It is important to identify and track each of the emerging sales opportunities at each account. Identifying specific opportunities provides much-needed feedback for tactical and strategic marketing. This feedback enables the marketing tacticians and strategists to validate their initial assumptions about the accounts and the potential applications within those accounts.

When opportunities are identified and tracked through the selling cycle, valuable information is available to field salespeople, sales

Opportunity Tracking		Created 6/3/95		Last Revised: 6/3/95	

Summary

Opportunity	Product Line	Product	Quantity	$ (K) Value	Estimated Close
Load Control	Notebook	Model m	550	1375	2/96
Security Mgmnt	Notebook	Model o	660	1500	3/96

Ongoing Sales Strategy: Created: 6/3/95   Last revised: 6/3/95

Load control
Currently on-track with the selling cycle. Prior to the negotiation step, we want to have our tactical marketing people make a presentation about our planned BBS and how the latest drivers can be accessed from the field. We also want to present how we are working with the major utility companies to adopt our algorithms for load control and utility savings.

Security Management
Also on-track with the selling cycle. We could experience a delay from the customer's perspective as they still don't have UL approval for their internal circuitry. I think it would be helpful if we could have a couple of engineers meet with their engineers and share with them how we got UL approval in record time. We can also arrange for tactical marketing to present an overview of Project Aegis.

Competitor Information:

Bergdorf Analytics
Currently seen as overall top supplier. They are focused on serving the upscale housing market with their custom-designed notebooks. Their engineering is strong and their quality is excellent. They hold the major SOP and will be a formidable competitor. Where we have a real chance is using the remote system checkout that marketing added to the product lines' features. This solves a major field support issue for them. Bergdorf is working on a similar approach but won't have it ready for this purchase decision.

Adelphi Systems
Handheld portables have been their strong suit in the past. They still hold a strong position, but they made some early mistakes in approaching this new area because they thought that they had the answers and didn't build the necessary relationships with the engineering and technical people. They are learning quickly and could be a major player in the future.

Exhibit 16.4

Opportunity Tracking and Ongoing Sales Strategy

management, and marketing planners. The salesperson, for example, benefits by being able to schedule personal selling time more effectively and to project commission levels. Also, knowing the unit and dollar potential of each opportunity plus its step in the selling cycle allows the salesperson to quickly generate an accurate bookings forecast.

Sales managers know where each and every sales opportunity is in its selling cycle and can use that information to report to senior management their confidence in making their quarterly performance goals. Tracking the sales opportunities also provides a rich database for comparing the performance of salespeople across territories and product lines, as well as in reviewing staffing levels needed to achieve specific sales goals.

One problem area can emerge during quarterly account reviews; the potential of micromanaging the salespeople. This problem can be avoided by summarizing sales opportunities during the quarterly reviews and making detailed reviews of specific activities a part of the ongoing interaction between sales managers and salespeople. This also helps prevent the quarterly reviews from bogging down in excruciating levels of detail. The salesperson reports the opportunities as shown in Exhibit 16.4, including the answers to the following questions:

- Where are we in the selling cycle?
- Have the key recommenders and decision makers been identified?
- Have we agreed on their specific needs and wants?
- Is the project funded?
- What is the timeline for a decision?
- Have we defined and agreed on the decision criteria?
- Do the criteria favor us? Why?
- What are the customers' objections?
- Have key people seen the demo?
- What is our next step? When? What are the expected results?

Ongoing Sales Strategy

In the ongoing sales strategy report, the salesperson describes his or her strategy for moving forward at the account, drawing on the discussion about the specific sales opportunities, and where they are in the selling cycle in determining the expected close date of the sale. Ongoing sales strategies may focus largely on following the selling cycle. On the other hand, if special meetings or additional opportunities are required to complete the sale, these plans are described. Exhibit 16.4 provides a brief example of how the ongoing sales strategy report might look.

Conducting Account Reviews

Target account review meetings are chaired by sales management. The intent of the meeting is not to dredge up the past and discuss reasons why sales opportunities were or were not closed as planned. Participants should instead focus on the near term and evaluate what must occur for the identified sales opportunities to be closed as planned. Salespeople are expected to come prepared and to present only those opportunities that have been identified and are being tracked through their respective selling cycles.

Preferably, the target account reviews will have been prepared electronically and made available to all interested parties before the meeting. This saves a lot of time and allows the participants to focus the limited time and resources on the more critical accounts. Sales management should prioritize the reviews and schedule the presentation order based on importance and need.

If the reviews are held on-site in a conference-room setting, participants should make provisions for messages to be taken and returned at specific times rather than permit unscheduled interruptions. When the reviews are generated electronically, it also is possible to conduct the reviews via video conferencing. One option is to connect all the participants on a conference call and then use groupware software to connect all participants to a main server containing the account reviews. The participants can then follow along on their own computers as the account information is presented. This method saves travel time and expense and accommodates any number of participants regardless of their location.

Coordinating Effective Action

Multiple groups and multiple functions are involved and participate in target account reviews. Sales, tactical marketing, and strategic marketing representatives are the primary participants, but other groups such as operations or finance management may also take part. Multiple perspectives provide the opportunity for breakthrough thinking through dialogue between these participants.

A real advantage of quarterly account reviews is the opportunity they provide for the coordination of effective action through agreed-upon strategies. Agreeing on proposed strategies and coordinating subsequent activities is a real plus. The target account review process provides a wonderful opportunity for achieving the primary goal of moving each of the identified and tracked opportunities forward in the selling cycle.

Chapter 17

Business Won/ Business Lost Analyses

The purpose of business won/business lost analyses is to evaluate the effectiveness of the entire account development cycle with an eye toward improving sales effectiveness. The analysis begins by focusing on the sales portion of the account development cycle and should, therefore, be chaired by sales management aided by the tactical marketing group. If, and when, problems emerge with product line features or served markets, the marketing tacticians bring them to the attention of the strategic marketing group.

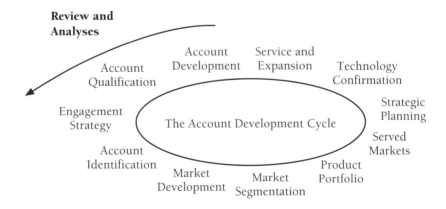

Exhibit 17.1

The Role of Review and Analyses in the Account Development Cycle

A key part of the account development cycle, (Exhibit 17.1), the analysis proceeds in reverse order starting with account service and expansion and progressing through account development, account qualification, engagement strategy, and so on. It usually begins by reviewing the contents of the sales kit and how the kits are being employed in the account development process. At each step in the cycle, participants ask what is working well and what is not. The goal, naturally, is to do more of what is working well and less of what is not. These discussions should take a balanced approach, covering both successful and unsuccessful features. Dwelling only on what didn't work can be counterproductive.

The Market by Product by Opportunity Matrix

One effective way of organizing business won/business lost data is to construct a matrix that shows an overview of the markets served, the product lines involved, number of sales opportunities identified, number completed, and percentages won and lost. For discussion purposes, we will use the previously introduced example of a computer manufacturer serving various markets with three major product lines. Exhibit 17.2 illustrates how these data can be presented.

Usually, more information is available about each of the opportunities than can be used effectively. The task is to select a level of detail that is meaningful and understandable without overwhelming the reader. Most of the insight will come from an understanding of the timing and competencies demonstrated at each step in the selling cycle, the effectiveness of the engagement strategy, contents and use of the sales kit, and the method used to identify prospective accounts. It is also possible that there are fundamental flaws in the product lines or that the served markets have been ill defined.

The first thing to look for is overall patterns in the data. This broader, macro view can be used to formulate hypotheses and construct follow-up questions about what might be happening. For example, looking at the matrix in Exhibit 17.2, we notice that servers are underrepresented in terms of number of sales opportunities identified.

Business Won/Business Lost Summary:				June 1995
		Major Product Lines		
	Totals	Notebook	Desktop	Server
All Markets				
No. Identified	324	125	153	46
No. Completed (%)	240 (74)	90 (72)	118 (77)	32 (70)
Won (%)	166 (69)	53 (59)	90 (76)	23 (72)
Lost %	74 (31)	37 (41)	28 (24)	9 (28)
Manufacturing				
No. Identified	125	35	75	15
No. Completed (%)	100 (80)	28 (80)	60 (80)	12 (80)
Won (%)	68 (68)	16 (57)	42 (70)	10 (83)
Lost (%)	32 (32)	12 (43)	18 (30)	2 (17)
Banking				
No. Identified	84	40	28	16
No. Completed (%)	62 (74)	32 (80)	16 (57)	14 (88)
Won (%)	34 (55)	12 (38)	12 (75)	10 (71)
Lost (%)	28 (45)	20 (63)	4 (25)	4 (29)
Legal				
No. Identified	115	50	50	15
No. Completed (%)	78 (68)	30 (60)	42 (84)	6 (40)
Won (%)	64 (82)	25 (83)	36 (86)	3 (50)
Lost (%)	14 (18)	5 (17)	6 (14)	3 (50)

Exhibit 17.2

Analysis of Business Won and Lost by Market, Product, and Opportunity

For those identified, however, the number completed is consistent with the completion rates in other categories. A closer look indicates that the number of server opportunities is also fairly constant across the three different served markets. We would expect that the opportunities would be much greater for the manufacturing and banking markets than for the legal market simply because there are more companies in each of those kinds of companies. A follow-up question would be to ask marketing tacticians about their expectations for the server product line. Are we under-identifying the sales opportunities, or are there just fewer of them because of the newness of the server applications?

Continuing to look at the total, we notice that we are completing 74 percent of the identified opportunities, on average, which is acceptable for now. In the future we want to increase that to a minimum of 80 percent, but we first want to increase the business-won rates across the board. Another follow-up question would be to look at the detailed selling cycle data to determine whether we underestimated the time required to complete the cycle, or whether we need to add some support staff to help the field salespeople. Looking at the pattern across markets and product lines, we notice that desktop applications in banking and server applications in the legal market account for the majority of opportunities not completed. We make a mental note to look more closely at these data during the detailed analyses.

Most important is the significant decrease in the number of sales opportunities won for the notebook product line across three out of the four served markets. This is worrisome as the notebook product line is intended to replace desktops as our primary source of revenue. We can compare the configuration of the *opportunities won* versus the configuration of the *opportunities lost* to see if there is any discernible pattern between the two.

Opportunities Won/Opportunities Lost Analysis

We can dig into the details a bit more and ask what we know about the opportunities won or lost? What was the average size of each opportunity in units? How were the products configured? Is the configuration pretty much as marketing forecast, or are we experiencing accelerated changes in the marketplace demand? Exhibits 17.3 and 17.4 provide a useful starting point for looking at the pattern of opportunities won or lost organized around how the product lines were configured for each of the served markets.

Opportunities Won: Manufacturing				June 1995
	Major Product Lines			
	Totals	Notebook	Desktop	Server
All Markets				
No. Identified	324	125	153	46
No. Completed (%)	240 (74)	90 (72)	118 (77)	32 (70)
Won (%)	166 (69)	53 (59)	90 (76)	23 (72)
Lost %	74 (31)	37 (41)	28 (24)	9 (28)
Manufacturing				
No. Identified	125	35	75	15
No. Completed (%)	100 (80)	28 (80)	60 (80)	12 (80)
Won (%)	68 (68)	16 (57)	42 (70)	10 (83)
Characteristics				
CPU				
486DX 66	10	–	10	–
Pentium 75	24	4	20	–
Pentium 90	34	12	12	10
unit buy				
<100	10	–	–	10
>200 <400	28	16	12	–
>400 <600	30	–	30	–
>600	–	–	–	–
configuration				
8MB RAM	10	–	10	–
8MB-16MB	20	–	20	–
>16MB	38	16	12	10
hard drive				
520MB	20	16	4	–
520-720MB	10	–	10	–
>720MB	38	–	28	10

Exhibit 17.3

Opportunities Won Analysis

For example, in Exhibit 17.3, Opportunities Won: Manufacturing, shows that the majority of the opportunities involved the newer Pentium processors, totaled between 400 and 600 units bought, had 8 or more megabytes (MB) of RAM, and were configured with fairly large hard drives.

On the other hand, Exhibit 17.4 indicates that most of the lost opportunities seem to have centered around products configured as 486s with 8MBs of RAM and smaller capacity hard drives. One question would be to ask if the sales kits are emphasizing the new Pentium chips at the expense of the older 486 chips. If they are, then we would want to review with marketing and decide whether we want to continue to focus on the new chips or redesign our sales kits to emphasize the older 486s for those customers who still want them. This is an important area to emphasize because tactical marketing's conversion plan (from 486 to Pentium) could be affected by changes in the marketplace. If we are introducing these changes due to the content of our sales kit and the focus of our salespeople, then we will want to review these areas and determine if our assumptions are still valid. These comments and observations pertain to both notebook and desktop product lines.

An additional question would be to ask whether the mix in opportunities won versus lost is consistent across the major sales areas. Exhibit 17.5, for example, illustrates that the numbers are fairly consistent across the different sales areas, so the issue is not attributed to any specific sales territory.

Once the sales areas have been reviewed, it is appropriate to look at the distribution of sales opportunities generated by the various salespeople both overall and on an area-by-area basis. These reviews can be helpful for the salespeople and for the area managers, who review the activity and success ratios for each salesperson. More creative companies may want to include statistics such as these in their sales compensation plans. For example, a salesperson could be given a financial incentive for increasing the number of opportunities completed or increasing the successful close ratio.

To illustrate how the data could be formatted, we will look at a comparison between the Midwest and West sales areas for the desktop product line. From Exhibit 17.5, note that each sales area enjoyed a

Opportunities Lost: Manufacturing				June 1995
		Major Product Lines		
	Totals	Notebook	Desktop	Server
All Markets				
No. Identified	324	125	153	46
No. Completed (%)	240 (74)	90 (72)	118 (77)	32 (70)
Won (%)	166 (69)	53 (59)	90 (76)	23 (72)
Lost %	74 (31)	37 (41)	28 (24)	9 (28)
Manufacturing				
No. Identified	125	35	75	15
No. Completed (%)	100 (80)	28 (80)	60 (80)	12 (80)
Lost (%)	32 (32)	12 (43)	18 (30)	2 (17)
Characteristics				
CPU				
486DX 66	26	12	14	–
Pentium 75	4	–	4	–
Pentium 90	2	–	–	2
unit buy				
<100	32	12	18	2
>200 <400	–	–	–	–
>400 <600	–	–	–	–
>600	–	–	–	–
configuration				
8MB RAM	26	12	14	–
8MB-16MB	4	–	4	–
>16MB	2	–	–	2
hard drive				
520MB	16	12	4	–
520-720MB	14	–	14	–
>720MB	2	–	–	2

Exhibit 17.4

Opportunities Lost Analysis

Opportunities Won/Lost by Sales Area: Manufacturing June 1995

	Totals	Notebook	Desktop	Server
		Major Product Lines		
All Markets				
No. Identified	324	125	153	46
No. Completed (%)	240 (74)	90 (72)	118 (77)	32 (70)
Won (%)	166 (69)	53 (59)	90 (76)	23 (72)
Lost %	74 (31)	37 (41)	28 (24)	9 (28)
Manufacturing				
No. Identified	125	35	75	15
No. Completed (%)	100 (80)	28 (80)	60 (80)	12 (80)
Won (%)	68 (58)	16 (57)	42 (70)	10 (83)
Lost (%)	32 (32)	12 (43)	18 (30)	2 (17)
East				
No. Identified	45	15	25	5
No. Completed (%)	36 (80)	12 (80)	20 (80)	4 (60)
Won (%)	25 (69)	7 (58)	15 (75)	3 (75)
Lost (%)	9 (31)	4 (42)	4 (25)	1 (25)
Midwest				
No. Identified	35	10	20	5
No. Completed (%)	28 (80)	8 (80)	16 (80)	4 (80)
Won (%)	22 (79)	4 (50)	15 (94)	3 (75)
Lost (%)	6 (21)	4 (50)	1 (6)	1 (25)
West				
No. Identified	45	10	30	5
No. Completed (%)	36 (80)	8 (80)	24 (80)	4 (80)
Won (%)	21 (58)	5 (63)	12 (50)	4 (100)
Lost (%)	17 (42)	5 (37)	12 (50)	0 (0)

Exhibit 17.5

Analysis of Opportunities Won and Lost by Sales Area

good opportunity identification and completion rate for desktops. There is, however, a striking difference in the percentage of business won. The Midwest won 94 percent of its opportunities while the West only won 50 percent of its opportunities. What was the distribution by salesperson for the two areas and what can we learn from that? Exhibits 17.6 and 17.7 illustrate these data.

The data in Exhibit 17.6 indicates that Patricia Ruggero is far and away the Midwest expert in identifying and successfully closing desktop sales opportunities. Bill Logan and Leonard Ross each have problem areas. For example, Bill may have trouble identifying opportunities, but once identified, he seems to be able to close them. We do not know this for sure, however, because the sample size is too small. But it is something that we should continue to study.

Leonard, on the other hand, seems to be having difficulty both in identifying and in closing opportunities. Leonard is a new hire who has not yet completed his training. We would schedule him for review next month and then follow-up to see how he is doing.

The data in Exhibit 17.7, on the other hand, present a different picture. Bill Hargraves is identifying most of the sales opportunities, but he is also accounting for most of the lost business. Some hypotheses might by that Bill is rushing through the selling cycle and not spending sufficient time to develop a relationship with potential customers. The other two salespeople may be spending too much time or perhaps not looking ahead to identify their opportunities. Both of these situations would benefit from additional analyses.

Sales Effectiveness Analysis

Whenever several salespeople are involved, there will be different levels of performance. The idea is to identify, analyze, and understand the sales processes followed by those salespeople who have different levels of success.

One effective approach is to choose a measure such as number of opportunities identified, number won, or number lost, to plot each salesperson's performance in the form of a distribution. A tight or

Opportunities by Midwest Area by Salesperson: Manufacturing			June 1995
	Major Product Lines		
	Totals	Notebook	Desktop	Server

Opportunities by Midwest Area by Salesperson: Manufacturing — June 1995

	Totals	Notebook	Desktop	Server
All Markets				
No. Identified	324	125	153	46
No. Completed (%)	240 (74)	90 (72)	118 (77)	32 (70)
Won (%)	166 (69)	53 (59)	90 (76)	23 (72)
Lost %	74 (31)	37 (41)	28 (24)	9 (28)
Manufacturing				
No. Identified	125	35	75	15
No. Completed (%)	100 (80)	28 (80)	60 (80)	12 (80)
Won (%)	68 (68)	16 (57)	42 (70)	10 (83)
Lost (%)	32 (32)	12 (43)	18 (30)	2 (17)
Midwest				
No. Identified	35	10	20	5
No. Completed (%)	28 (80)	8 (80)	16 (80)	4 (80)
Won (%)	22 (79)	4 (50)	15 (94)	3 (75)
Lost (%)	6 (21)	4 (50)	1 (6)	1 (25)
P. Ruggero				
No. Identified			16	
No. Completed (%)			14 (88)	
Won (%)			14 (100)	
Lost (%)			0 (0)	
B. Logan				
No. Identified			3	
No. Completed (%)			1 (33)	
Won (%)			1 (100)	
Lost (%)			0 (0)	
L. Ross				
No. Identified			1	
No. Completed (%)			1 (100)	
Won (%)			0 (0)	
Lost (%)			1 (100)	

Exhibit 17.6

Analysis of Opportunities Won and Lost in the Midwest Area by Salesperson

Opportunities by West Area by Salesperson: Manufacturing	Major Product Lines			
June 1995	Totals	Notebook	Desktop	Server
All Markets				
No. Identified	324	125	153	46
No. Completed (%)	240 (74)	90 (72)	118 (77)	32 (70)
Won (%)	166 (69)	53 (59)	90 (76)	23 (72)
Lost %	74 (31)	37 (41)	28 (24)	9 (28)
Manufacturing				
No. Identified	125	35	75	15
No. Completed (%)	100 (80)	28 (80)	60 (80)	12 (80)
Won (%)	68 (68)	16 (57)	42 (70)	10 (83)
Lost (%)	32 (32)	12 (43)	18 (30)	2 (17)
West				
No. Identified	45	10	30	5
No. Completed (%)	36 (80)	8 (80)	24 (80)	4 (80)
Won (%)	21 (58)	5 (63)	12 (50)	4 (100)
Lost (%)	17 (42)	5 (37)	12 (50)	0 (0)
B. Hargraves				
No. Identified			20	
No. Completed (%)			14 (70)	
Won (%)			4 (29)	
Lost (%)			10 (71)	
D. Willetts				
No. Identified			5	
No. Completed (%)			5 (100)	
Won (%)			4 (80)	
Lost (%)			1 (20)	
M. McGoldrick				
No. Identified			5	
No. Completed (%)			5 (100)	
Won (%)			4 (80)	
Lost (%)			1 (20)	

Exhibit 17.7

Analysis of Opportunities Won and Lost in the West Area by Salesperson narrow distribution indicates that the salespeople are pretty much doing the same thing. A loose or wide distribution, however, provides ample opportunity for an overall performance boost for all salespeople. In a wide performance distribution, the difference between the performance of the salesperson at the low end versus the high end of the distribution is on the order of two to three times! That means if you can understand what the salesperson at the high end is doing to be so successful and you can help those at the low end increase their performance, sales effectiveness can be increased as much as 30 to 50 percent.

These detailed analyses will involve digging into specific salespersons' selling cycles and reviewing how they approach their prospective customers. Additional discussion of these methods, however, is beyond the scope of this book.

To make the best use of the analysis, only the top three reasons for lost opportunities should be summarized and reported. It is helpful to review these reasons within the context of the account development cycle and to analyze the following aspects of the top three:

1. Account development (use of the selling cycle)
2. Account qualification (relationships)
3. Engagement strategy

Other analyses may indicate different reasons for opportunity loss. For example, product features may be different than those requested, the price may be too high, delivery may be late, or quality may not meet expectations. Using the account development cycle, however, these issues appear less and less because the salesperson is truly qualifying and developing the account.

Feedback to Marketing

Within the context of the relational model, tactical marketing is involved throughout the business won/business lost analyses. Remember, the goal is not to find fault but to discover new opportunities. In the illustration of the Midwest and West sales areas, marketing tacticians would recognize the need to train the salespeople in how to use the databases and how the overall process should work. Sales management and marketing tacticians may also want to review the effectiveness of the sales kits and how the salespeople are introducing them to customers.

Chapter 18

Standard Software Tools

One of the most difficult tasks in using the relational model and the account development cycle is to tie the various marketing and sales functions together, electronically, in a way that creates cooperation and collaboration, not confusion and conflict. Personal computers are widely used in virtually all businesses. Their use, however, is often driven by a mundane need such as the hiring of a single new employee or one specific capability such as e-mail, spreadsheets, or word processing.

Few companies, for example, have a vision of how current information technology can be applied to improve their internal business practices and operations. It is true that many companies are purchasing notebook and laptop computers for their salespeople, and some companies even use electronic data interchange (EDI) to reduce paperwork, lower inventories, and shorten the order-entry cycle. Few, however, are looking to see how their various business processes can be tied together electronically to increase the quality and speed of information flow between marketing strategists, marketing tacticians and the sales organization.

Integrated Applications

Two leading standard software packages go a long way toward tying the marketing and sales organizations together. These two packages are Microsoft Office and Lotus SmartSuite/NotesSuite. Together, they account for the majority of the integrated Windows applications market. Integrated applications exchange information through software technology such as Dynamic Data Exchange (DDE) and Object Linking and Embedding (OLE). Microsoft Office includes Excel (spreadsheet), PowerPoint (presentation graphics), Access (relational database), and Microsoft Mail. These powerful programs work well together, but they do not offer the corporatewide benefits of Lotus Notes.

Lotus NotesSuite is really an extension of Lotus's SmartSuite integrated applications and is designed to support the sharing of knowledge rather than simply the exchange of data. NotesSuite is designed to support both the sending and sharing of information useful to marketing and sales. Any information put together by marketing planners can be immediately accessed by salespeople as well as other interested parties.

An Example: Lotus NotesSuite

Lotus NotesSuite is billed as the only groupware suite of software products for team collaboration. It basically combines Lotus Notes with SmartSuite; the collection of applications covering 1-2-3 spreadsheets, Ami Pro word processing, Freelance Graphics presentation, and Approach relational database. The personal information manager, Organizer, is also contained in SmartSuite.

Lotus Notes/FX (Field Exchange) is the technology that allows Lotus's suite of desktop applications to share data fields and thereby extend the power of both Notes and the desktop applications. With Notes/FX, marketing and sales personnel can both have immediate access to centrally stored account profiles, sales kits, and contact reports. NotesSuite is also ideal for the field salesperson who may be operating out of a home or mobile office.

Lotus NotesSuite extends the power of the integrated applications by making each desktop a Notes-compatible system. For example, Lotus Notes is client/server software that can be used by a group of users to share information across a network. The client is the user's PC, desktop or notebook, with a copy of Notes client software installed. The server is also a PC with Notes server software installed and is used as a data storage point. There can be several servers for different types of data and different user authorization. Servers can be accessed directly (network) or by remote call-in via modem. Several databases can be installed on a Notes server with each database serving the needs of specific work groups. Another real advantage of NotesSuite is that it is compatible across a mixed platform environment. Exhibit 18.1 illustrates the different operating systems on a common network.

The remainder of this chapter will lay out a vision about how standard software such as NotesSuite can be used rather than to describe how to create the various software elements. The discussion is organized around the relational model and the account development cycle. Exhibit 18.2 diagrams the relationship between strategic marketing, tactical marketing, and sales. A similar diagram can be used as a con-

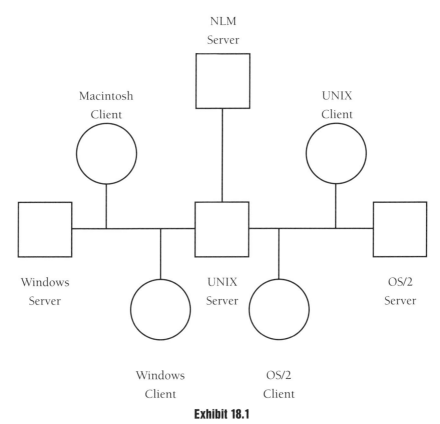

Exhibit 18.1

Simplified Network Showing Mixed-Platform Clients and Servers

Exhibit 18.2
Relational Diagram of Marketing and Sales

ceptual model for network servers and clients. For example, there can be specific servers for strategic marketing, tactical marketing, and sales with a central server serving the shared needs of all three functions.

There are five broad classes or categories of applications for which Notes is most suitable. The application classes are discussion, tracking, workflow, reference, and broadcast. Discussion applications refer to technical discussions, dialogue about new or planned products, and bulletin board discussions. This class would be appropriate for discussions about the effectiveness of sales kits, engagement strategies, and new product rollouts.

Tracking applications are used to identify and maintain the status of specific projects. They are useful in tracking on the status of sales opportunities on the development schedules for new products.

Workflow applications are used to automate tasks such as price quotes, requests for delivery dates, and expense report routing. Workflow applications are also useful in accessing backlog and shipping information for specific customers.

Reference applications are great for recording the strategic plan, as well as for developing sales kits. Press clippings and news releases could be added to the sales kits continuously and made available to authorized users. These applications can also be used to generate product data sheets. Marketing tacticians can then update their product line data sheets by simply modifying the master stored on the server.

Broadcast applications can be used for general company announcements, price changes, and other information suitable for a wide audience. Taken together, these five classes of applications thus tie together the information needs and wants of marketing strategists, marketing tacticians, and the sales organization.

The components of NotesSuite are powerful desktop applications in their own right. Couple these applications with Note/FX, however, and many additional benefits emerge. The major components of Notes/FX are briefly highlighted in the following sections.

Spreadsheet

Lotus 1-2-3 is a powerful spreadsheet program that allows you to organize and graph data in a wide variety of formats. The 1-2-3 templates can be set-up to facilitate the creation, review, approval, or rejection of tabular data such as marketing and sales forecasts. By embedding 1-2-3 spreadsheets as OLE (Object Linking and Embedding) objects within Notes documents and exchanging data via Notes/FX, applications of this type use the calculation capabilities of 1-2-3 and the information-sharing power of Notes. Forecasts generated by marketing planners become available to authorized others. When forecasts are revised, the changes are communicated to the others automatically. Spreadsheets can also be embedded in the target account reviews, and selling cycles can be created in 1-2-3.

Word Processing

Ami Pro is a word processing program that allows you to create documents that range from a basic letter to a full-blown business plan. You can create a dynamic business plan using Ami Pro and Notes/FX. All authorized people can have access to the business plan and revisions can be made as the marketplace changes. Critical sections can be embedded in other documents for use in strategic and tactical marketing reviews.

Target account profiles, competitor profiles, white papers, testimonials, and product data sheets can be created using Ami Pro and

Notes/FX and assembled into sales kits. Photographs, drawings, or spreadsheets can also be embedded in Ami Pro documents.

Database

Approach is a relational database that allows marketing and sales to work with multiple database files to assemble, organize, and report data designed to answer specific questions or to provide specific insight. For example, the marketing people might use an Approach application with Notes/FX to develop a quality database containing all failure analysis reports. When confronted with an unusual quality problem, any authorized user can access the database and query the records to determine if there is a larger problem than first reported.

An Approach database can also be used in identifying prospective target accounts. The universe of companies can be downloaded into the database and then searched using predetermined criteria. Business won/business lost records can also be maintained in an Approach database.

Presentation

Freelance Graphics (FG) is a powerful presentation program. A skilled person using FG can quickly create professional-looking presentations that include slides, overheads, handouts, and speaker notes. This application is a natural for creating the many different types of presentations required for engagement strategies. As new information is available, marketing tacticians can modify the presentations which, in turn, are available to salespeople via Notes/FX. This will eliminate obsolete presentations and all-night preparation by the salespeople as they try to create an up-to-date presentation for the next day's critical meeting.

FG also contains a time-saving organization chart tool. The user selects one of six different types of organization chart styles and enters the pertinent information. This tool is great for updating the account and competitor profiles.

PIM

Personal information manager (PIM) software is used by most sales-people today. Unfortunately, it is usually treated as the electronic equivalent of a "black book" and is seldom used to track sales opportunities through their selling cycles. SmartSuite's PIM Organizer is a powerful addition to a busy person's tool kit. It can track work and personal calendars, keep notes, and remind the user of appointments using adjustable alarms.

Account Development Cycle

We will now look at each of the steps in the account development cycle and comment on how NotesSuite could improve knowledge-sharing across the three functions. (Exhibit 18.3 shows the account development cycle.)

Strategic Planning

Within the context of the relational model and the account development cycle, strategic marketing is primarily responsible for the strategic plan. With Notes, various marketers can collaborate to produce a

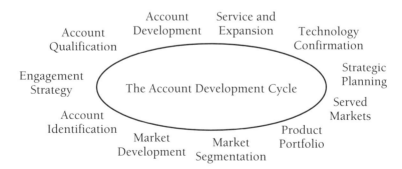

Exhibit 18.3

The Account Development Cycle

strategic plan over the network using Ami Pro. Specific people could prepare an outline to be completed by those individuals who are most knowledgeable of the topics. Revisions could be maintained including comments from the participants. Market research information could be linked to the plan and the plan is updated as the data change. The strategic planning process could thus be a truly dynamic process.

Served Markets

The definition of the served markets and the classification of the major needs and wants of each market served can be created and maintained in Ami Pro or 1-2-3. Criteria for selecting the markets to be served can be reviewed by all authorized users. News feed services can be linked to each served market document for automatic updating of relevant news.

Product Portfolio

The major product lines can be tracked in terms of their served markets. Product features and served market needs and wants can be stored in an Approach relational database. Relational databases permit effective searches using multiple two-dimensional data tables. Using such searches, the relationship between product features and benefits can be continually checked against the needs and wants of the served markets. The results of business won/business lost analyses can be linked to these data.

Market Segmentation

Market segmentation studies can be conducted and distributed in Ami Pro or Approach. Downloads for market research firms can compare total available market (TAM), served available market (SAM), and share of market (SOM) with field sales data regarding total account purchases (TAP), served account purchases (SAP), and share of account purchases (SOP). This provides an easy way to validate share of market including contributions of major accounts.

Market Development

Market development is the step in the account development cycle where primary responsibility shifts from marketing strategists to marketing tacticians. The various electronic databases could be accessed and the data downloaded into an Approach database to permit secondary searching and to make the basic data available to authorized users. News feeds could also be added to these databases. The criteria developed for use in the selection of prospective target accounts could be developed collaboratively.

Account Identification

The identification of prospective target accounts from the universe of existing companies is a key step in the account development cycle. If the accounts are misidentified, then revenue plans and profitability plans are thrown awry. Using an Approach database to apply the search criteria allows the marketing planners to identify prospective accounts quickly and accurately. An added advantage is that the criteria can be displayed for comment before selecting the accounts and thereby marketing can tap into the collective knowledge of all authorized users.

Once the prospective target accounts have been identified, the names can be cross-searched against the names of existing accounts to create the engagement matrix, and target account profiles and competitor profiles can be created in Ami Pro. At this time, the sales kits can be developed using Freelance Graphics, Ami Pro, and 1-2-3. Specialty templates can also be constructed for specific selling cycles for each of the major product lines, or simpler versions can be constructed in 1-2-3.

Engagement Strategy

The engagement strategy matrix functions as a sales call planner. Created in Ami Pro and Freelance Graphics, the matrix can be a useful guide for the salespeople as they prepare for the account qualification step in the cycle.

Account Qualification

Account qualification is the step in the account development cycle where primary responsibility shifts from marketing tacticians to the sales organization. The initial task of the salesperson is to use the prior work to develop an understanding of the prospective account. During the initial meetings, the salesperson wants to learn as much about the account's business as possible.

Downloading the sales kit with product and account information and reviewing the material before the first sales call is essential. The salesperson must learn about the customers' business by reviewing press releases or financials, and information on their products and served markets. The salesperson can then verify the information contained in the sales kit. Is the organization still structured as it is described in the sales kit? Have they had any new acquisitions? This information can be transferred to the Notes server and the sales kit updated.

Account Development

Following account qualification, specific sales opportunities can be defined during the account development process. It is at this point that the salesperson identifies and begins to track each of the sales opportunities through its respective selling cycle. This information can be tracked in 1-2-3 or it can be tracked in specially developed opportunity tracking templates. He or she can use Organizer as a personal information manager, to set appointments, keep notes, and maintain a personal address book.

What is so powerful is that once the sales opportunities are tracked and reported, sales management can generate a bookings forecast simply by searching the sales opportunities and knowing their step in their respective selling cycles. This means that the salesperson no longer guesses about customer demand. Forecasts are generated only from identified opportunities. With identified opportunities, sales management also knows product configuration, specific quantities, and customer. This is a great advantage in operations planning!

Service and Expansion

Ongoing service notes, returns, warranty claims, and quality problems can be recorded in a Notes database. Records of requested delivery dates versus scheduled dates versus actual ship dates, together with the number of reschedules, provides a useful database for reviewing the quality of customer service. With these data in an Approach database, cross searches by product line or major customer can uncover weak service areas. This type of information becomes very valuable when reviewing contractual performance.

Technology Confirmation

When business won/business lost analyses are maintained in a Notes database, discussions of technology confirmation, reaffirmation, or redirection become data based. The sales organization, for the first time, has a structured way of presenting the effectiveness of the technology from the perspective of the customer. These analyses can be linked with prior work on needs and wants of the served markets and compared against the features and benefits of the product lines.

The Present and Future

When marketing strategists take the lead and form the strategic plan, which identifies the served markets, defines the parameters for successful products, and segments the market, the result can be a well-focused company.

When marketing tacticians take responsibility for the identification of prospective accounts, your company automatically picks up a 15 to 20 percent increase in available selling time because you no longer require your field salespeople to prospect. Add to that the advantage to the salesperson of knowing about the account and the products being targeted and you will probably pick up another 5 to 10 percent in productive selling time.

Finally, when you eliminate the salesperson's monthly chore of generating a detailed forecast by part number by customer by month for the next six or twelve months, you've made a friend for life. Salespeople hate to generate forecasts. When you track each opportunity through its selling cycle, you generate the forecast automatically!

Tying the three functions together electronically, using nothing more than standard software, offers incredible benefits. But what if you do not want to invest in Lotus Notes or NotesSuite? With notebook computers and access to the Internet, sales kits can be constructed and distributed electronically, thereby standardizing sales presentations and eliminating the need for the salespeople to prepare their own presentation.

Product data sheets can also be posted to the Internet with each customer downloading and printing as many copies as needed. With this method, the huge inventories of outdated data sheets are eliminated as is the cost of printing them. Although much has been said recently about CD-ROM catalogs, it is better to put your product catalog and data sheets on the Internet and let interested parties access them directly. This prevents your customers' inadvertent use of an outdated version of the CD.

The Future

The future lies in the increased use of wireless technologies. Cellular data modems will transmit data using the existing cellular phone infrastructure and opportunity tracking can be updated shortly after meeting with the customer. Once again, the forecast is generated from the salesperson's opportunity tracking. The result should be more accurate forecasts with less work to produce them and more satisfied customers.

*A*ppendix

Case 1

Scorpio Sportswear

Scorpio Sportswear, a family business, is a brand-new start-up. George and Ann Carruthers, brother and sister, started the business a few months ago after returning to their childhood home for the holidays and commiserating with each other about the inequities of corporate life. In their early 40s each has worked for major garment manufacturers and major retailers. They know the intricacies of the business and are interested in developing and profiting from their ideas and creations. The first step to success, of course, is knowing the market and the needs and wants of potential customers. From their extensive industry experience, both Ann and George know what people want. They also know a lot about manufacturing costs and part of the uniqueness of their designs incorporates that considerable manufacturing knowledge into the end product. They plan to use their knowledge to source and purchase manufactured services rather than build a manufacturing plant themselves, thereby offering the potential for increased margins, if they can bring their designs to market quickly. Their products offer an unusual blend of style, color, quality, and durability and are targeted at the moderate to better consumer, male and female, who is active, fit, and concerned with a healthy lifestyle. They discussed their plans in general and then developed a more formalized plan. They are entirely self-funded.

Strategic Marketing

Scorpio's strategic plan focuses almost entirely on marketing because Ann and George have decided that they want a low overhead operation that consists basically of the two of them plus contract help as needed. Being self-funded, they are conscious about the need for sustained yet controlled growth.

Strategic Planning

Scorpio's strategic plan is generated in response to three broad questions:

- Where are we now?
- Where would we like to be by when?
- How do we get there?

The strategic plan consists mainly of the company's mission statement; some information about the industry and the macro trends that indicate why this is a good time to do what they are planning to do; definition and size of the markets they intend to serve and their target share; product portfolio; estimated product sales for each market segment served; and a projection of the revenue and profit contribution for each product line. These broad issues set the tone for the more detailed activities within the context of the account development cycle.

Served Markets

From the market data she included in the strategic plan Ann has identified that the annual U.S. market for 100 percent cotton moderate to better sportswear is about $2.4 billion and is growing at an annual rate of 12.5 percent. There are literally hundreds of competitors with no single company accounting for more than 1 percent of the market. This a niche market served by specialists.

Scorpio has identified a two-tiered niche market that they believe is underserved. Both tiers are to be served with all cotton, moderate-to-better active sportswear marketed with and through high-end vacation resorts and golf courses in the Southwest. The focus of this market is the upscale resorts and better golf courses, the majority of which are located in the geographic areas of Arizona, New Mexico, Southern California, and Southern Colorado, because the clientele match the profile of the customers George and Ann wish to serve.

Regional preferences are important. Ann's research has identified preferred activities by major geographical areas and has decided to segment served markets geographically by identified preferences.

For example, Arizona activities are dominated by golf and tennis during the day and in the evening, by small intimate social gatherings at trendy restaurants and clubs in the metropolitan areas. New Mexico activities involve skiing in the winter and attendance at concerts and visits to art galleries and pueblos and related Native American sites in the spring and summer. Evening entertainment is important in New Mexico, but the style and degree of formality is different from the Arizona communities of Phoenix, Scottsdale, and Tucson.

Southern California is also different. Golf and tennis prevail during the day but with a different flair than that of the Arizona communities. Styles tend to be less conservative and more avant-garde. Southern Colorado activities are dominated by hiking, horseback riding, and skiing. The styles tend to be more Western than Southwestern with a distinct preference for stylized cowboy attire. In Exhibit A1, Ann has laid out her view of how their served market is segmented.

Product Portfolio

From a strategic marketing perspective, Exhibit A1 contains an overview of the major product lines. Early research has indicated that people who buy moderate-to-better active sportswear at upscale resorts tend to purchase multiple tops to go with each pair of pants; whether short or long. A key selling point, therefore, is for colors to be compatible across a wide variety of styles which, in turn, invites the buyer to feel confident in purchasing multiple items. Any resort logos or stencils must be color fast and must be positioned on the garment so neither the style of the garment nor the logo are compromised.

Mission Statement: Scorpio Sportswear designs, markets, and distributes active sportswear to the major vacation resorts of the Southwest.

Industry Information: Worldwide, cotton denim is a $6.5 billion business. The U.S. accounts for roughly two-thirds of the total or approximately $4 billion. The U.S. Market is growing at an annual rate of approximately 9 percent.

Served Market: Our primary served market, 100 percent cotton moderate to better active sportswear, is currently a $2.4 billion market growing at an annual rate of 12.5 percent. This market is currently served by hundreds of small suppliers who market their goods through distributors and who are seldom the same suppliers from one year to the next. Turnover is high. We propose to serve a narrowly defined subset of this market, namely the upscale vacation resorts of the Southwest. We estimate this market to be somewhere between $800 million and $1.2 billion and growing at nearly 20 percent annually.

Macro Trends: Nationally, there has been a continued increase in the desire for natural fiber clothes. Cotton is the fabric of choice in the northern climes as it is used by the moderate to better buyer for tasteful layering and all weather functionality. Across the sunbelt, and especially in the American Southwest, 100 percent cotton garments are the preferred choice of the fashion conscious, fit, healthy, and active consumer. Our research has also shown it is these same affluent people who frequent the upscale resorts. Our plan is to use our creative designs and knowledge of the needs and wants of the consumer to partner with the resort management and offer our active sportswear exclusively through their facilities.

Segment	Arizona	Southern California	New Mexico	Southern Colorado
Golf	X	X		
Tennis	X	X		X
Hiking	X	X	X	X
Casual	X	X	X	X

Product Lines	Golf	Tennis	Hiking	Casual
Shorts	X	X	X	X
Long Pants	X	X	X	X
Tops	X	X	X	X
Windbreakers	X	X	X	X

Target SOM:	Golf	Tennis	Hiking	Casual
Year 1	0.1%	0.1%	0.1%	0.1%
Year 2	0.2%	0.2%	0.2%	0.2%
Year 3	0.4%	0.4%	0.4%	0.4%
Year 4	0.6%	0.6%	0.6%	0.6%
Year 5	0.8%	0.8%	0.8%	0.8%

Exhibit A1

Summary of Selected Elements of the Strategic Plan

Market Segmentation

Segmentation is planned to occur along the lines outlined in Exhibit A1.

Tactical Marketing

Ann and George design the specific garments, choose the colors, and develop the merchandising plan within the broad product line and market segment direction set by their strategic marketing plan. Weather conditions determine the busy season at the major resorts targeted, so they arrange their market development activities to occur well ahead of the peak season, usually September to May. Many resorts are training staff in late August and early September, so targeting their sales calls early in August is preferred.

Market Development

Tactically, Scorpio will focus on the Arizona market with specific emphasis on Phoenix and the surrounding Valley of the Sun and the Greater Tucson area. Within these two metropolitan areas, there are about 50 upscale resorts and more than 300 golf courses, which represents about 80 percent of Scorpio's market. The product lines selected are the golf and tennis shorts, tops, and long pants in combination earth tones and bright colors.

Aware that Scorpio is not a big name and concerned that prospective accounts will not give them the time of day, Ann and George decide to create a national advertising campaign. They both know Elizabeth Darden, the host of the PBS series "Four Star Resorts." They contact Elizabeth, describe their new business plans, and offer to provide free sportswear to her in return for mentioning Scorpio on the air. Elizabeth likes the idea and suggests that they should also consider providing samples to resort management and resort professionals.

Account Identification

Criteria for the identification of target accounts include upscale resorts that share the following criteria: rates greater than $200 per night; 500 rooms or more; and adjacent golf and tennis facilities with resident professionals. Their preliminary search turn up 30 prospective accounts. George and Ann decide to focus on the top 20 revenue producers in the Phoenix area and the top 10 producers in the Tucson area. Letters are sent to resort management and ownership with follow-up calls to arrange a meeting with the resort's buying staff and golf and tennis professionals.

Engagement Strategy

Scorpio Sportswear is a new company offering new products to the marketplace. One of its initial hurdles is to build credibility that it is a viable and dependable company and is in business for the long haul. George and Ann prepare a series of slide presentations that include some of their major accomplishments and a sampling of design awards earned before founding Scorpio. They also will use this presentation to build an interesting story for the founding of Scorpio.

George and Ann's presentation to resort management will focus on financial strength, integrity, automated ordering and overnight restocking, customer service, and sales training for resort staff. Then they will prepare slides of their initial products and explain how these products fit in with their overall market development plans (both the current and future year's lines). Specifically, they will describe how much shelf space is required and what sort of revenue and margin could be expected from each major product line per unit of shelf space. Finally, they prepare sample packets of each of the major product lines so they can demonstrate how they can be mixed and matched across all colors and styles.

Sales

During this initial phase of the company's activities, Ann and George will handle the direct sales. They will use the different slide presentations, testimonials, style sheets, photographs, and samples as their sales kit. Their goal is to schedule a series of meetings with the management of the 30 targeted companies over a period of 10 days. The purpose of these initial meetings will be to review the resorts' facilities, understand the needs and wants of resort management, and discuss how the two companies might work together. Based on the outcome of these initial meetings, some orders may be taken during the first visit while others will require a second call. Some resorts may be locked into prior agreements and will not want to discuss things further. Reviews of opportunities won and lost after each sales call will help sharpen the focus of future contacts.

Both of the founders are experienced merchants but even the most experienced merchants sometimes miss what will sell. As an added incentive, Ann and George explain their "wide and shallow followed up with narrow and deep" approach to merchandising. Simply stated, the initial "wide and shallow" activity places a wide selection of styles, colors, and sizes but with a smaller number of each piece. The resort shops monitor sales and their point-of-sales (POS) system is automatically polled electronically to monitor which styles, colors, and sizes are selling the best. An initial replacement order is generated automatically for twice the initial quantities and shipped via Fedex for delivery by 10:00 am the following morning. This automatic polling continues with automatic reorders based on actual sales. As soon as the rate of increase in sales drops off, the reorder rate drops off as well. This unattended sales monitoring and automated reordering process almost guarantees to resort management that they will not be stuck with unsold merchandise.

Subsequent account reviews will use the automated polling and reorder rates to fine-tune the system. New styles, models, colors, and sizes can be adjusted based on demographics and sales performance. Peak day and time of day buying patterns can be detected and proshop staffing adjustments made accordingly. With an accurate and up-to-date database, customers can be matched across other criteria and followed-up with an upscale mail order catalog.

Case 2

Karatchi and Karatchi Legal Services

Karatchi and Karatchi is a Washington-based legal firm specializing in intellectual property issues for for-profit corporations. Five years ago the firm's founding partners, Rudy and Tanya Karatchi, left successful careers with established firms to set out on their own.

They have not looked back. Annual revenue has grown from nothing to $5 million in year 5. Their client base is spread across a variety of industries doing both domestic (U.S.) and international business. The industries include cosmetics, pharmaceuticals, and healthcare; microelectronics, computers, and software; and forestry products and industrial machinery. Their areas of representation have focused on copyright law, import/export-related business transactions, and transportation of toxic materials.

Business has been very good—almost too good. A number of forces have made their specialties growth areas, and the Karatchi's are stretched about as far as possible under the present circumstances. They are faced with a choice: either expand to be able to take advantage of the growing demand for their services (and maintain the same level of quality) or stop growing and miss out on a great opportunity.

They decide to expand. Their first hire is an old friend and colleague, Bill Spence, who, in addition to having complementary legal expertise, is a "rain-maker" skilled in new business or practice development. Bill looks at the Karatchi and Karatchi financials and notes that, despite their excellent growth, there is one serious lack: no strategic plan. He sets about to develop one.

Strategic Marketing

Marketing can be a difficult activity for attorneys. While most wish to proactively carry their message to prospective clients, they are limited by ethical rules and guidelines. These rules and guidelines are less stringent than in the past, but most advertising by attorneys is still associated with "ambulance chasing," and, in the market served by the Karatchi's, is frowned on in the extreme. Thus, the first strategic issue is communicating with a market without directly "selling" to it. The second, of course, is the traditional one: identifying and estimating potential.

Strategic Planning

In beginning to develop a strategic plan, Spence addresses two questions:

1. How will the firm communicate with prospective clients in a professional manner?
2. What will the target market be?

Spence first looks at the firm's revenue distribution for the current year:

		in 000's
Cosmetics		500.0
Pharmaceuticals		600.0
Healthcare		900.0
Microelectronics		800.0
Computers		600.0
Software		1,000.0
Forestry		300.0
Industrial Machinery		300.0
Total		5,100.0

Spence concludes (and the Karatchi's agree) that the firm should deepen the market penetration of the broad markets they already serve.

Spence finds the answer to the other question—how to reach the market—in a single word familiar to attorneys: collegiality. In marketing terms this translates into an image marketing or public relations/publicity program. This kind of program would respond to professional considerations, involve the firm's active participation in the professional activities of the target markets served, and would give the firm visibility and a positive reputation in its served markets.

In the strategic planning process Spence sizes the total available market (TAM) for legal services in the U.S. at approximately $75 billion. Given that the U.S. accounts for somewhere between two-thirds and three-quarters of the world's attorneys, we would add about an additional $25 billion for non-U.S. based legal services, bringing the annual world market for legal services to about $100 billion. See Exhibit A2.

Mission Statement: Karatchi and Karatchi provide legal services to business organizations active in domestic and international commerce. Legal support of business transactions is a specialty.

Organization: Karatchi and Karatchi is organized into the legal equivalent of strategic business units (SBU). The eight SBUs are: pharmaceuticals (PHM), microelectronics (ME), computers (COM), software (SOFT), cosmetics (COS), forestry products (FOR), healthcare (HC), and industrial machinery (IM).

Total Market: The total available market (TAM) for legal services is estimated at $75 billion annually for the U.S. and approximately $100 billion worldwide.
Served Market: Karatchi and Karatchi's served available market (SAM) is defined as business transaction law and is estimated at $4 billion and growing at an annual rate of 20 percent. The current services by SBU is shown below.

Service/SBU	PHM	ME	COM	SOFT	COS	FOR	HC	IM
IPR/Tech	X	X	X	X	X	X	X	X
Joint Vs	X	X	X	X	X	X	X	X
Intl Com	X	X	X	X	X	X	X	X
Litigation	X	X	X	X	X	X	X	X
BODs	X	X	X	X	X	X	X	X

Proj Revenue	Year 1	Year 2	Year 3	Year 4	Year 5
All SBUs	$7.25mm	$9.38mm	$11.06mm	$13.59mm	$17.39mm

Exhibit A2
Summary Plan for Karatchi and Karatchi

Spence makes note of two additional items for the future. He notes that eventually an operating budget for the image marketing program will need to be developed to account for the cost of printing, distribution, attendance at industry programs and so forth. Also, he groups industries served into Strategic Business Units (SBUs). At present this is probably more organization than needed, but it helps identify specific markets and market needs and also gives the firm a structure for future growth.

Served Markets

Karatchi and Karatchi's served available market (SAM) consists of domestic and international business transactions estimated to be between 3 and 5 percent of the total available market of $3 to $5 billion. This SAM is growing at an annual rate of 20 percent that is being fueled by several converging trends:

1. The decline of communism and the spread of capitalism.
2. The explosion in worldwide commerce driven by the Internet and the rapid adoption of wireless telecommunications.
3. The tendency for companies to collaborate or form joint ventures to pursue market opportunities rather than "go it alone."
4. The interest and desire of many companies to look for and hire, on a temporary or project-oriented basis, the most qualified resources available rather than hire permanent employees.

Service Portfolio

To serve its market, the firm offers legal services to address such issues as defining and maintaining copyright law for information published on the Internet and broadcast throughout the world; understanding how to operate within the confines of various country's tariffs and import/export duties and licenses, creating and administering international letters of credit, advising and structuring domestic and international cross-licensing agreements; advising on royalty payments, establishing, educating, and advising boards-of-directors; and advising on the appropriate ways of selling and/or transporting toxic materials across international borders.

Business transaction law encompasses all of these areas but does not necessarily involve direct litigation. Although Spence and the Karatchi's are experienced with direct litigation, they have decided that, as a firm, they will not offer these services but will act in an advisory capacity or help manage major litigation for clients. Direct litigation can be very time-consuming and can strain the resources of a small, three-member firm, such as K & K.

Within the business transaction market, Spence divides the firm's service portfolio into five major strategic business units (SBUs): intellectual property rights and technology licensing; joint ventures; international commerce; litigation advisory services; and advisory boards/boards-of-directors. These SBUs and their estimated revenue contributions for year 1 are detailed in Exhibit A3. The total revenue for years 2 through 5 are shown for reference. As each year's planning cycle approaches, the next year's revenue projection can be updated. Although it is too early to do so now, at some point in the future, each SBU defined will be headed by a partner.

Market Segmentation

Spence could segment the firm's market in a couple of different ways, but he chooses to segment based on the needs and wants of the marketplace.

Building on their fundamental strengths in intellectual property law, Spence segments the firm's served market into eight broad industry categories: pharmaceuticals, microelectronics, computers, software, cosmetics, forestry products, healthcare, and industrial machinery. The service by segment matrix is shown in Exhibit A2.

Market Development

Market development involves publicizing and positioning the firm in each of its served market segments, which for K & K means being knowledgeable about the companies it serves and the customers those

Service/SBU	PHM	ME	COM	SOFT	COS	FOR	HC	IM	Totals
IPR/Tech	$0.1	$0.3	$0.7	$0.2	$0.5	–	–	$0.2	$2.00
Joint Ventures	–	$0.1	–	$0.7	–	–	–	$0.5	$1.30
Intl Commerce	$0.2	–	$0.1	–	$0.7	–	–	$0.5	$1.50
Litigation	$0.5	$0.1	$0.5	–	–	–	$0.1	–	$1.20
BODs	$0.5	–	$0.5	–	$0.1	–	$0.15	–	$1.25
Year 1 Totals	$1.3	$0.5	$1.8	$0.9	$1.3	–	$0.25	$1.2	$7.25

Service/SBU	PHM	ME	COM	SOFT	COS	FOR	HC	IM	Totals
IPR/Tech									
Joint Ventures									
Intl Commerce									
Litigation									
BODs									
Year 2 Totals									$9.38

Service/SBU	PHM	ME	COM	SOFT	COS	FOR	HC	IM	Totals
IPR/Tech									
Joint Ventures									
Intl Commerce									
Litigation									
BODs									
Year 3 Totals									$11.06

Service/SBU	PHM	ME	COM	SOFT	COS	FOR	HC	IM	Totals
IPR/Tech									
Joint Ventures									
Intl Commerce									
Litigation									
BODs									
Year 4 Totals									$13.59

Service/SBU	PHM	ME	COM	SOFT	COS	FOR	HC	IM	Totals
IPR/Tech									
Joint Ventures									
Intl Commerce									
Litigation									
BODs									
Year 5 Totals									$17.39

Exhibit A3

Revenue Contribution by Service Category by SBU

companies serve. Spence lists the following questions. What are the major industry events that companies in each segment would not be caught dead missing? To what industry associations do they belong? What are the key legislative issues facing the companies in each segment? Are there barriers to international trade? Are punishing tariffs or duties being imposed? For each company engaged in international trade, how do the citizens of those countries view actual or prospective client companies? Questions like these create the basic ideas for market development efforts.

Spence outlines a plan for market development on several levels. First, articles on free trade or the need for tariff reform will be written by the firm's members and published in the magazines and journals read by prospective clients in target industries. Members of the firm will participate in industry study groups or other forums devoted to major issues facing the respective targeted industries. A review of the literature for each major segment will identify the major issues facing each segment. The firm can then respond to one or more topics in print or host a conference to discuss them. The outcome of this activity will be one or more white papers or position papers discussing critical issues facing the relevant industries. These papers will be sent at no charge to the heads of the major companies and to their board members.

In more specific terms, the firm plans to initiate the following publication program. They will prepare a series of books and booklets about the critical legal issues facing the companies in each of the firm's defined segments. They also have their own Web Page on the Internet and will use it as a source of leads. For qualified leads, they will distribute electronic abstracts of their books and articles free of charge. They also will speak at industry trade shows, association meetings, and international conferences and publish their speeches or presentations on the Internet.

Account Identification

The first level of identification uses the broad segments such as pharmaceuticals, software, and so on. The criteria to be used in identifying specific prospective accounts will depend on the market segment

Target Account Profile	Created: 10/23/95 Last Revised: 11/11/95

Name and Location:

Becker Pharmaceuticals, Inc.	Ownership: Public
8500 N. Becker Drive	Formed: 1897
Watertown, MA 02172	Annual Sales: $7855mm
Phone: (617) 555-5900	No. of Employees: 65,000
Fax: (617) 555-0520	

Company Description:
Parent/holding company with high-tech operating units involved in biotechnology, medical systems, pharmaceuticals, and chemical measurement systems.

Product SIC Codes:	**Key Personnel:**
6719 Holding/parent company	William Gruendig, President and CEO
	Carol Trattoria, VP Marketing
	Abbey Cohen, VP Finance and CFO
	Phil Blackberg, VP Engineering
	Robert Lemoux, VP Sales

Our Principal Competition:
1st: Bigelow and Cocopelli (Intellectual Property)
2nd: Smalle and Winters (Litigation Services)

Exhibit A4

Account Profile

served. For example, for one category of pharmaceuticals Spence wants to identify prospective accounts greater than $100 million in revenue *and* active in cross-license agreements with companies in Latin American countries. For another category of pharmaceuticals, he will wish to identify companies that are greater than $500 million in revenue and have joint ventures with companies in Eastern Europe. He differentiates because the legal needs of the two groups of prospective accounts are different. The process of identifying prospective accounts continues for each of the eight segments. An example of a target account profile is shown in Exhibit A4.

The "sales kit" is a virtual kit, and not a single physical entity. It will feature copies of relevant publications. In addition, it will include collateral or supporting materials intended to present the capabilities of the firm, the credentials of the partners, and specific knowledge and understanding of the issues. It also will contain some information about fee-based services and how the firm is generally engaged. Similar content will be on the firm's Web Page. The sales kit is electronic and is constructed specially for each prospective account targeted.

Engagement Strategy

The engagement strategy will be different for each prospective account. For new accounts, the engagement strategy involves either direct or indirect referral. Direct referrals come from current satisfied clients. These clients, of course, will be sent copies of articles developed and published by the firm. This adds a level of complexity to the account development cycle because you now must be aware of the major referral sources and how you can develop them just as you would develop a target account.

Indirect referrals can be developed by the kinds of contacts that companies in the targeted markets have with the firm's work. One is through the firm's publications. Another is through professional resource groups (basically groups of professionals who share common interests) formed by the firm. Each senior partner will sit on and, in some cases, chair two or more of these resource groups, which will be made up of top executives from the leading companies in each market segment.

Although few attorneys like to refer to their efforts to obtain new clients as sales, that is exactly what K & K's activities will be. When marketing and sales are viewed as a relational process within the context of the account development cycle, sales does not consist of cold calls or a scattered approach to contacting prospective clients. It involves the process of calling on identified prospective accounts, understanding their issues, and collaboratively agreeing on how your services can satisfy their needs. Spence has developed a "selling cycle" for new clients that will work well for the firm. (Exhibit A5).

Step	Cumulative Probability of Close	Elapsed Time in Weeks
1. Initial contact	0.1	Start
2. First call/follow-up	0.2	2.0
3. Discuss broad opportunities	0.3	4.0
4. ID/specific opportunity	0.5	6.0
5. Meeting re: general approach	0.6	9.0
6. Introduce SBU partners	0.7	12.0
7. Joint presentation to client	0.8	15.0
8. Letter of engagement	0.9	21.0
9. Close/agree to proceed	1.0	26.0

Exhibit A5

Selling Cycle for Karatchi and Karatchi

Sales

Only the senior partners in Karatchi and Karatchi (Rudy and Tanya Karatchi and Jim Spence) are involved in direct sales. Each is scheduled to call on three new prospective accounts each week. From prior experience they have learned that the ratio of new accounts contacted to new business closed is about 30 percent. This differs sharply from other law firms where the ratio, if monitored at all, is more like 5 percent. Their experience with the selling cycle indicates that there is an average elapsed time from initial contact to close of new business of about twenty-six weeks. They also monitor the average revenue generated per client for each segment and use that information in their sales call planning.

Account qualification is less of an issue for Karatchi and Karatchi because their leads come from legal issues reflected in their image marketing program. Prospective clients will have responded to the firm's publications and thus will have self-defined their concerns and needs. If a client company has retained an attorney for certain legal matters, it does not mean that other attorneys won't also be retained.

Karatchi and Karatchi offer legal management services so it is possible that the client company may want K&K to manage the attorneys they have previously retained.

Staying on Track

Staying on track refers to how well the actual revenue is tracking on the planned revenue. The firm will conduct traditional target account reviews to compare plans and actual performance. Every other month, the senior staff meet and review each of the target accounts. The partner

---

Target Account Review   Created: 10/23/95   Last Revised: 11/11/95

Name and Location:

Becker Pharmaceuticals, Inc.	Ownership: Public
8500 N. Becker Drive	Formed: 1897
Watertown, MA 02172	Annual Sales: $7855mm
Phone: (617) 555-5900	No. of Employees: 65,000
Fax: (617) 555-0520	

Company Description:
Parent/holding company with high-tech operating units involved in biotechnology, medical systems, pharmaceuticals, and chemical measurement systems.

Product SIC Codes:	**Key Personnel:**
6719 Holding/parent company	William Gruendig, President and CEO
	Carol Trattoria, VP Marketing
	Abbey Cohen, VP Finance and CFO
	Phil Blackberg, VP Engineering
	Robert Lemoux, VP Sales

Our Principal Competition:
1st: Bigelow and Cocopelli (Intellectual Property)
2nd: Smalle and Winters (Litigation Services)

Exhibit A6

Account Review

Business Conditions & Position Created 11/11/95 Last Revised: 11/11/95

Current Business Conditions:
Becker Pharmaceuticals is the parent/holding company for approximately 25 different operating companies engaged in biotechnology research and pharmaceutical manufacturing. For the past 5 years, they have spent approximately $6 million per year in legal services and appear to be on track for the same level of spending this year.

Position at the Account:
At the present time, the prestigious European law firm of Brandt, Burghausen, and Weiner are servicing the parent company but they are looking for U.S. law firms with which to build strategic alliances. They are specifically interested in working with us in the areas of intellectual property rights and litigation services. We are scheduled to meet with two of the senior partners early next quarter.

Projected Revenue (in thousands of dollars):

	Forecasts		
Service Category	**1996**	**1997**	**1998**
Intellectual Property Rights	200	400	650
Litigation Services	550	750	1200
Total	750	1150	1850

Near-Term Strategy:

We are still early in the selling cycle. We have identified the broad opportunities where we can work together and our next meeting is with two of the senior partners, and if successful, will move us to a probability level of 0.6. Assuming all continues to go well, we could be looking at new business in about 2 or 3 quarters.

Exhibit A7

Current Business Conditions and Your Position at the Account responsible for the account leads the discussion and explores with the other partners such topics as business conditions at the account, status of the active work, revenue to date, costs associated with the account, contact notes, and plans for the immediate future.

Business Won/Business Lost Summary:		November 1995	
		Major Service Category	
	Totals	Intellectual Property	Litigation Services
All SBUs			
No. Identified	12	10	2
No. Completed (%)	3 (25)	2(20)	1 (50)
Won (%)	2 (67)	1 (50)	1 (100)
Lost (%)	1 (33)	1 (50)	0 (0)
Pharmaceuticals			
No. Identified	8	6	2
No. Completed (%)	2 (25)	1 (17)	1 (50)
Won (%)	1 (50)	1 (100)	0 (0)
Lost (%)	1 (50)	0 (0)	1 (100)
Software			
No. Identified	2	2	–
No. Completed (%)	1 (50)	1 (50)	–
Won (%)	1 (100)	1 (100)	–
Lost (%)	0 (0)	0 (0)	–
Healthcare			
No. Identified	2	2	–
No. Completed (%)	0 (0)	0 (0)	–
Won (%)	0 (0)	0 (0)	–
Lost (%)	0 (0)	0 (0)	–

Exhibit A8

Analysis of Business Won and Lost by Service Category by SBU

Also every other month, the partners meet and review the status of their sales efforts. Like the target account reviews, each partner presents those accounts with whom he or she has been working, where they are in the selling cycle, and when they can expect to close. At these same meetings they also discuss any new business that has been won or lost. Exhibits A7 and A8 illustrate how account data is organized.

Business Won/Business Lost Analyses

Each quarter, the senior partners meet to discuss new sales opportunities that are emerging for each service category and SBU. The purpose will be to review the number of sales opportunities identified, number completed, percent won, and percent lost. It is through the process of business won/business lost analyses that the firm will find the greatest insight into the pulse of the business. For example, Exhibit A8 shows that there has been no activity for the service category of litigation services for either the software or healthcare SBU. Does this suggest that there is no activity or does it suggest that one of their competitors is identifying and winning the business. For the other two SBUs, they note that while there have been a substantial number of opportunities identified, a smaller than desirable number have been completed. This suggests too little time is being spent to develop new business.

McGregor's Specialty Meats

McGregor's is a second-generation privately owned family business supplying specialty processed meats to supermarkets, institutions, and restaurants. The company has grown steadily over the years by supplying hot dogs and quality ground beef patties to long-term customers at a reasonable price. In the early days, there was not much need for strategic planning because they could always sell more than they could make. In the past few years, however, the company has been experiencing some difficulties, which has prompted the new president, Bob McGregor, to do some serious thinking and ask some difficult questions. Bob is asking questions such as:

- What do we know about our customers?
- What are the key trends?
- What do our customers want from us that can help them better serve their customers?
- What are the products in which they are most interested?
- What does customer service mean to them?
- What selling price and cost structure do we need to make a reasonable profit?
- Who is our competition?
- What are their strengths and weaknesses?
- How should we be organized to better serve our customers?

These questions have led to a series of meetings with the senior management of the company. They are interested in implementing a strategic planning process that is customer-responsive, flexible in form, and somewhat informal in appearance.

Strategic Marketing

McGregor's Specialty Meats is faced with some unique issues. Its processing plant is 50 years old, although in reasonably good shape. Quality ground beef patties and hot dogs have been their primary products, but recent changes in eating habits have negatively affected their hot dog sales, and aggressive pricing by major group beef suppliers has threatened their ground beef sales. It is time to act.

Strategic Planning

Bob is sensitive to the fact that the company has never really had a strategic plan, and he knows it is long overdue. He knows his staff well and believes the key to effective planning lies in a process that is flexible and collaborative rather than rigid or mechanical. He is convinced that if he is actively involved and takes a leadership role in the planning process other key people will participate as well.

Bob is especially sensitive to the need to protect the current business while crafting a plan to move McGregor's into new markets. He decides the first order of business is to hold an in-depth review of current accounts to review any issues that might jeopardize their current business while developing a plan to position the company to participate in new markets. He asks Jim Wilson, his sales manager, to chair the meeting and provides him with an outline of the topics he would like addressed. A copy of Bob's memo to Jim is shown in Exhibit A9.

Jim meets with his sales people and together they design a two-page format that addresses Bob's requirements. Jim's sales people are up-to-date on the issues at their accounts, so the information requested is easily gathered and organized during a couple of half-day meetings. An off-site meeting is scheduled with senior management from finance,

September 5, 1995

To: Jim Wilson   cc: staff
From: Bob McGregor
Subject: Account Reviews

As you know, I have been thinking about the need for us to have a strategic business plan that includes a much longer look ahead than what we have done historically. At the same time, I am concerned about jeopardizing our current business.

I want you and your salespeople to pull together some information on our current accounts and lead a discussion with me and the rest of the staff so we know the status of each account and what we feel collectively has to be accomplished to protect our current business. This should give us the short-term focus we need.

Prepare your reviews using the following structure:
1. Brief history of how the account was obtained and how long they have been an account
2. Primary market served by the account
3. Current overall importance to McGregor's (10 point scale, 1 not at all, 10 essential)
4. Sales history in pounds for last 5 years by product line
5. Major competitors at the account
6. Open issues at the account
       Price
       Quality
       Delivery
7. Recommended action plan to address open issues
8. Six-month forecast (pounds) by product line by month

Please let me know when you will have these reviews completed. Also, I would like each review to be two pages maximum. When you are ready, I will schedule an offsite with my staff.

Thanks,

Bob

Exhibit A9

Memo from Bob McGregor

marketing, sales, operations, and administration in attendance. Jim leads the discussion using the account review format he and his staff developed. An example of the format used is shown in Exhibit A10.

From these account reviews, a host of issues surrounding the three key areas of price, quality, and delivery emerged. A list of action items with specific responsibilities assigned followed the meeting. Confident that the account review process has provided the attention and short-term focus required, Bob's attention turns to thinking about the longer term. What is to be McGregor's focus?

Reflecting on the account review meeting, Bob concludes that McGregor's future success lies in servicing the multiple needs and wants of their customer base better than any other supplier—in other words, deepening their existing market rather than broadening it. He decides to develop his strategic plan around the concept of improved service and concludes that their mission statement should reflect that belief.

Served Market

McGregor's serves the specialty processed meat needs of restaurants, hotels, schools, supermarkets, delicatessens, and institutions. It offers only specialty seasoned and cooked meats. It does not sell raw meat products.

The *total available market* (TAM) for processed meats is estimated at $23 billion and is growing at an annual rate between 3 and 5 percent. Processed meats includes canned meats, sausage products, frankfurters, bacon, boiled ham, baked ham, salt pork, pickled pork and so on. Sausage products and meat snacks account for about $10 billion annually.

McGregor's served available market (SAM), a subset of the total market, is defined by three major cooked beef product lines: roast beef, corned beef, and pastrami. This SAM is approximately $1 billion and, after of a number of years of single-digit annual growth, began growing recently at an annual rate of 12 percent. McGregor's current revenue of $50 million puts their share of market (SOM) at 5 percent. As a general strategy, Bob wants to maintain McGregor's market share at between 5 and 7 percent, which means his near-term growth rate

Account Review: November 8, 1995

Account Name and Location:
Westwind Foods, Inc.
1287 E. Cicero Place
Los Angeles, CA 95012

Affiliation:
Low cost distribution arm of
Giant Foods

History:
Customer since 1985. Came to us when their supplier dropped them for not paying their bills within 30 days. Bob Sr. helped Bill Eccles out of a pinch and they have been a good customer ever since.

Primary Served Markets:
They are a big player in the institutional and school markets. They serve probably 60 percent of the private nursing home market and about half of the schools in the western states.

Importance to McGregor's (1 to 10 with 10 essential): 9

Sales History Last 5 years only
(thousands of pounds):

	1994	1993	1992	1991	1990
Roast Beef	350.	285.	245.	220.	195.
Corned Beef	150.	120.	110.	100.	95.
Pastrami	75.	65.	60.	60.	58.
Total	575.	470.	415.	380.	348.

Major Competitors:
For roast beef it is Clover Foods
For Pastrami and Corned Beef it is Riscoe Distributors

Open Issues at the Account:
Price: We are in good shape. We just announced a 3 cent per pound reduction which places us about mid-range in the price distribution. Clover is lower by 1 cent and Riscoe is actually higher by a penny.
Quality: Our packages have ripped a few times in the past few months but otherwise OK.
Delivery: Here is where we can really improve. Of the last 100 orders, we have shorted them an average of 2 cases per order. We usually make it up within a day or so but not without a hassle.

Recommended Action Plan:
Nail down the delivery issues. It looks like the issue is our planning yields are higher than what we've been running. Adjust the yields and we should be OK.

Six Month Forecast by Product Line
(thousands of pounds):

	Dec	Jan	Feb	Mar	Apr	May
Roast Beef	30.	32.	32.	34.	35.	36.
Corned Beef	12.	12.	14.	14.	16.	16.
Pastrami	6.	6.5	7.	7.5	8.	9.
Total	48.	50.5	53.	55.5	59.	61.

Exhibit A10

Existing Account Review

must meet or exceed slightly the growth rate of the SAM: 12 percent annually. This becomes useful information when reviewing installed capacity and creating next year's capital budget.

Product Portfolio

The company's main product lines are roast beef, corned beef, and pastrami, which are forecast to continue as is but with some additional fragmentation into different packages and different flavor profiles. For example, under Bob's leadership, a richer flavor profile was developed for McGregor's line of delicatessen corned beef. This has resulted in McGregor's corned beef dominating the delicatessen markets in all major metropolitan areas. People who have eaten McGregor's corned beef in one or more of the national chain of delicatessens have praised the quality and the flavor. It is Bob's intent to capitalize on this reputation and develop additional products each with a unique flavor profile. He intends to leverage his approach to service through increased new product development.

Market Segmentation

McGregor's markets are segmented horizontally and defined as restaurants, hotels, supermarkets, delicatessens, and institutions. Accurate processed meat numbers are difficult to obtain for specialty product lines. An alternate approach is to estimate the company's share of the total volume of goods purchased of each product line. Buyers are usually comfortable providing this information. An estimate of

Share-of-Purchases (SOP)	Created 11/8/95		Revised: 11/8/95		
Products/Segments	Restaurant	Hotel	Supermarket	Delicatessen	Institution
Roast Beef	0.5%	0.6%	1.0%	2.0%	0.5%
Corned Beef	0.2%	1.0%	2.0%	1.0%	0.5%
Pastrami	0.5%	1.0%	1.0%	4.0%	0.5%

Exhibit A11
Estimated Share-of-Purchases (SOP) by Product Line by Market Segment

share-of-available purchases (SOP) by product line by market segment is shown in Exhibit A11.

Tactical Marketing

Market Development

Being a relatively small company, McGregor's strategic and tactical marketing responsibilities are handled by Jim Wilson, the head of marketing and sales. Jim is well aware of the differences between strategic marketing, tactical marketing, and sales and does an excellent job of balancing the three functions. For Jim, tactical marketing involves implementing the marketing strategies developed previously, which includes developing a sales kit consisting of trade show materials, product data sheets, testimonials, white papers on meat processing, and articles publicizing new and more sanitary food handling practices. With the exception of the trade show materials and booth, all materials are available electronically.

Markets are developed and served via a combination of direct salespeople and wholesale food representatives. Wilson's views are that the direct salespeople serve more as target account managers and work with the representatives to develop account development strategies. They partner with wholesale representatives and develop a combined strategy for penetrating and servicing the target accounts.

McGregor's approach to market development over the years has been to be active in the various trade shows where the company's salespeople can meet and interact with existing and prospective customers. It is not uncommon for an existing customer to introduce or refer a prospective customer based on the quality of the product and interest in service. It is this approach to market development that has convinced Bob McGregor of the need to continue and intensify McGregor's record of fine service.

Account Identification

Wilson identifies prospective target accounts through a set of successive criteria. The first criterion is financial stability. It begins the evaluation process by requesting a credit report using one of the on-line credit services. Once the credit check is completed favorably, the next criterion is current and projected product consumption rate in pounds per week. Over the years, McGregor's has learned that its most successful customers purchase between 3,000 and 10,000 pounds per week. Wilson prefers to start small and understand the subtle preferences of each new account and then slowly increase weekly ship quantities.

Engagement Strategy

Wilson believes in a personalized and somewhat low-keyed approach to account development and has trained his direct sales force in this approach. For new accounts, it involves arranging a personal visit to present the credentials of the company and to understand the general interest level and desires of the customer. For existing accounts interested in expanding their business or accounts which McGregor's has targeted for expansion, different engagement strategy is warranted. The potential issues may involve price, quality, or delivery, so McGregor's salespeople are prepared to engage around any of the issues presented. They prepare for meetings by obtaining actual records for price, quality, and delivery and review them in detail before calling on the account. They are also authorized to commit the company to certain actions based on their meeting with the customer. Please refer to the selling cycle, in Exhibit A12, for a review of the major steps in McGregor's approach to engaging, qualifying, and developing their target accounts.

Step	Cumulative Probability of Close	Elapsed Time in Weeks
1. Initial contact	0.1	Start
2. First call/follow-up	0.2	2.0
3. Send company brochure	0.2	3.0
4. Follow-up call/samples	0.4	5.0
5. Customer visit/second sample	0.6	8.0
6. Present price and delivery	0.7	10.0
7. Special packaging/labeling	0.8	12.0
8. Single trial order	0.9	14.0
9. Close/receive volume order	1.0	16.0

Exhibit A12

Selling Cycle for McGregor's Specialty Meats

Sales

Account Qualification

Although account qualification is often referred to in the context of new accounts, it is also a relevant concept for existing accounts. For example, if McGregor's is interested in increasing its share of purchases (SOP) at the account, it must begin by understanding the pressures of the customer's business and reviewing basic needs and wants within that context. Sales reps need to ask questions about the nature of the business, what is working well and what is not, how McGregor's products help or do not help. Reps make no assumptions about additional business being due them because they are a current supplier. They follow the same steps of the selling cycle for new business.

Account Development

Once the necessary relationships have been built and the basic needs and wants understood within the context of the customer's business, the salesperson seeks to identify specific opportunities that McGregor's products can satisfy. The account development process has at its foundation, the fundamental understanding of the customers' business. For example, when calling on an institutional account, factors that are important are consistency of product, shelf life, flavor profile, appearance, and cost. In many cases cost may appear to be an overriding concern, but, in fact, products that are cost-effective are more important than products with the lowest cost. Thus, low trim losses, consistent quality, opportunity for customized weights, and special packaging all contribute to a cost-effective solution. When the salesperson understands the needs of the business and can present products within that context, he or she has an increased chance for a successful sale and a satisfied customer. Once again, this is part of Bob's concept of service.

Service and Expansion

Service and expansion involves continued service and the sales of additional product if appropriate. For example, a large chain of Dixie Stores in the Southeast has been buying McGregor's roast beef, but not corned beef or pastrami. On a recent visit, Jim Wilson was reviewing McGregor's on-time delivery status with Dixie's senior buyer, Taft Heidegger, and at the conclusion of the review, Jim commented that there might be an opportunity for Taft to increase cooked meat sales at his 150 stores by offering a corned beef special that corresponds with St. Patrick's Day.

After some discussion, Jim suggested that Taft place a 15,000-pound order, packaged in 25 pound cases, with delivery scheduled about 5 days before the holiday. Jim further suggested that Taft sample the product wide and shallow; in other words, place 100 pounds of corned beef in all 150 stores. This would minimize Taft's exposure in the event their customers do not buy the product and would give Jim an opportunity to observe which stores sold the product out the fastest. Jim also indicated to Taft that McGregor's would implement electronic ordering and guarantee shipment of an additional 15,000 pounds within 12 hours of receipt of that order. Taft agreed and gave Jim the order. The trial was a success, and a second 15,000-pound order was placed and delivered. Subsequently, Dixie placed an order for

260,000 pounds of corned beef subject to weekly releases of 5,000 pounds each over the next year.

Technology Confirmation

This section is normally thought to relate only to the high-tech companies where exotic technologies and manufacturing processes are used to manufacture a sophisticated product. However, McGregor's Specialty Meats also uses technology, in their case to prepare and process the meat products including creating special seasoning recipes, trimming and tying the meat, cooking methods and cycles, cooling, packaging, and in-process controls for contamination.

The salesperson plays a vital role in this process as they are the ones who observe the product in the customers' stores, schools, restaurants, and institutions. They are sensitive to how the product looks, how it survives the delivery process, and how it presents when positioned adjacent to a competitor's product. To facilitate the information-gathering process, McGregor's has equipped all of their salespeople with notebook computers, wireless modems, and digital cameras. When they are at the customer's site, they are encouraged to take photos of competitors' products and transmit them to headquarters with their comments. Their trip notes are stored in a Notes database and accessed by marketing and operations.

Staying on Track

Structured account reviews were used to initiate the process of strategic planning, and they are also used to help McGregor's stay on track or, better, yet, get back on track when they stray. McGregor's uses ongoing quarterly account reviews using the following format to stay on track:

• Account name and location

• Current business conditions at the account

• McGregor's position at the account

• Sales history

Account Review: November 8, 1995

Account Name and Location:
Westwind Foods, Inc.
1287 E. Cicero Place
Los Angeles, CA 95012

Affiliation:
Low cost distribution arm of
Giant Foods

Current Business Conditions:
Business is up about 6 percent this year over last year. They are automating their warehouse and order entry system which is helping them increase their inventory turns by about 50 percent. Stores on their distribution routes are doing well with all of the new construction. Look for about a 10 percent increase in total sales to Westwind this year.

McGregor's Position:
We continue to be their supplier of choice. Ever since Bob Sr. helped out Bill Eccles, we keep getting as much business as we can handle. Recent delivery problems have raised the competitive issue with the new people. We are developing a campaign for our pastrami. See opportunity below.

Sales History Last 5 years only (thousands of pounds):

	1994	1993	1992	1991	1990
Roast Beef	350.	285.	245.	220.	195.
Corned Beef	150.	120.	110.	100.	95.
Pastrami	75.	65.	60.	60.	58.
Total	575.	470.	415.	380.	348.

SAP:
Basically, we have all of their business.

Opportunity:
We presented a merchandising plan to increase the quantity of pastrami. We published some new sandwich recipes and joined their salespeople on sales calls to the supermarkets and institutions.

We are looking at an initial order for 25,000 pounds and if that moves like we think it will, they will follow-up with a standing order for about 15,000 pounds per week. Probability about 0.8.

Competition is not an issue. This business is ours to lose.

Next Quarter's Sales Strategy:
Close the incremental pastrami business.

Quarterly Bookings Forecast by Product Line (thousands of pounds):

	Q1
Roast Beef	90.
Corned Beef	40.
Pastrami	20.
Total	150.

Exhibit A13

Sample Account Review

- Served available purchases (SAP)
- Share of Purchases (SOP)
- Opportunity defined and positioned in the selling cycle
- Competitor information
- Next quarter's sales strategy

An example account review is shown in Exhibit A13.

Business Won/Business Lost

McGregor's business won/business lost analysis is an essential step in its relational approach to marketing and sales. The reviews are held quarterly with marketing, sales, operations, and finance in attendance. Decisions to modify the contents of the sales kit are often made on the spot with a commitment from the responsible individual when the modifications will be available. It is also not uncommon for this process to generate ideas for new products or ways to modify existing products. McGregor's reviews are structured and reported to correspond with their market segments. For example, rather than reporting by geographical area, reports are conducted by segment: restaurant, hotel, school, supermarket, delicatessen, and institution. Exhibit A14 illustrates how these reviews are structured.

One example of information generated by the business won/business lost summary was the school market. There had been little activity in this area, and the opportunity that was identified was lost. The analysis did not show what the issues are; for example, committee member did not know whether the salespeople did not call on the accounts or if they did and there are no opportunities available. A detailed follow-up meeting was scheduled to pursue these questions and get answers to them.

Business Won/Business Lost Summary: Q3 '95		October 9,1995		
	Major Product Lines			
	Totals	Roast Beef	Corned Beef	Pastrami
All Segments				
No. Identified	21	10	5	6
No. Completed (%)	12 (57)	5 (50)	3 (60)	4 (67)
Won (%)	6 (50)	1 (20)	2 (67)	3 (75)
Lost (%)	6 (50)	4 (80)	1 (33)	1 (25)
Restaurant				
No. Identified	8	6	1	1
No. Completed (%)	2 (25)	1 (17)	1 (100)	0
Won (%)	2 (100)	1 (100)	1 (100)	0
Lost (%)	0	0	0	0
Schools				
No. Identified	1	1	–	–
No. Completed (%)	1 (100)	1 (100)	–	–
Won (%)	0	0	–	–
Lost (%)	1 (100)	1 (100)	–	–
Supermarkets				
No. Identified	4	1	1	2
No. Completed (%)	2 (50)	1 (100)	0	1 (50)
Won (%)	1 (50)	0	0	1 (100)
Lost (%)	1 (50)	1 (100)	0	0
Delicatessens				
No. Identified	4	1	1	2
No. Completed (%)	3 (75)	1 (100)	0	2 (100)
Won (%)	2 (67)	0	0	2 (100)
Lost (%)	1 (33)	1	0	0
Institutions				
No. Identified	4	1	2	1
No. Completed (%)	4 (100)	1 (0)	2 (100)	1 (100)
Won (%)	1 (25)	0 (0)	1 (50)	0
Lost (%)	3 (75)	1 (100)	1 (50)	1 (100)

Exhibit A14

Business Won/Business Lost Summary

Index

American Marketing Association

The American Marketing Association, the world's largest and most comprehensive professional association of marketers, has over 40,000 members worldwide and over 500 chapters throughout North America. It sponsors 25 major conferences per year, covering topics ranging from the latest trends in customer satisfaction measurement to business-to-business and services marketing, to attitude research and sales promotion. The AMA publishes 9 major marketing publications, including *Marketing Management*, a quarterly magazine aimed at marketing managers, and dozens of books addressing special issues, such as relationship marketing, marketing research, and entrepreneurial marketing for small and home-based businesses. Let the AMA be your strategy for success.

For further information on the American Marketing Association, call TOLL FREE at 1-800-AMA-1150.

Or write to
American Marketing Association
250 S. Wacker Drive, Suite 200
Chicago, Illinois 60606
(312) 648-0536
(312) 993-7542 FAX

TITLES OF INTEREST IN MARKETING

For further information or a current catalog, write:
NTC Business Books
a division of NTC Publishing Group
4255 West Touhy Avenue
Lincolnwood, Illinois 60646–1975 U.S.A.